Front View of the President's House in the City of Washington

THE WHITE HOUSE

ACTORS AND OBSERVERS

Edited by William Seale

NORTHEASTERN UNIVERSITY PRESS • *Boston*

Northeastern University Press

Copyright 2002 by The White House Historical Association

Library of Congress Cataloging-in-Publication Data
The White House : actors and observers / edited by William Seale.
p. cm.
Essays derived from papers delivered at a 200th anniversary symposium sponsored by the White
House Historical Association.
Includes index.
ISBN 1-5553-547-X (alk. paper)
1. White House (Washington, D.C.)—History—Congresses. 2. White House (Washington, D.C.)—
History—Pictorial works. 3. Presidents—United States—Congresses.
4. Presidents—United States—Pictorial works. 5. Presidents—United States—Family—
Congresses. 6. Washington (D.C.)—Social life and customs—Congresses. I. Seale, William.
II. White House Historical Association.
F204.W5 W57 2002
973´.09´9—dc21

2002009087

Designed by Gary Gore

Composed in Bembo by Gary Gore. Printed and bound by Friesens Printers,
Altona, Manitoba. The paper is Luna Matte, an acid-free stock.

MANUFACTURED IN CANADA
06   05   04   03   02   5   4   3   2   1

Frontispiece: *The President's House, 1807*, from Charles William Janson,
The Stranger in America (London: Albion Press, 1807).

The White House Historical Association is a nonprofit organization chartered November
3, 1961, to enhance understanding, appreciation, and enjoyment of the Executive Mansion. All
proceeds from the trusts of the White House Historical Association and from the sale of its
publications and products are used to fund the acquisition of historic furnishings and artwork for
the permanent White House Collection, assist in the preservation of the public rooms, and further
its educational mission. For more information visit www.whitehousehistory.org.

To Robert L. Breeden

Chairman, 1990–2000,

White House Historical Association

Contents

Color Plates

Contributors

CATHERINE ALLGOR received a Ph.D. from Yale University and specializes in women's history in the early American republic. She is editor of the Louisa Catherine Johnson Adams (Mrs. John Quincy Adams) Papers at the Massachusetts Historical Society and the author of *Parlor Politics: In Which the Ladies of Washington City Help Build a City and a Government.*

JEAN BAKER, professor of history at Goucher College, is director of the undergraduate program in historic preservation. She received a Ph.D. from Johns Hopkins University and has taught at the University of North Carolina and Harvard University. Her study of political culture, *Affairs of Party,* won the Berkshire Prize in 1983, and her *Mary Todd Lincoln* received the Willie Lee Rose Prize in 1987.

ALLIDA BLACK, research professor of history at George Washington University, is director and editor of the Eleanor Roosevelt Papers. She received a Ph.D. from George Washington University. Her books include *What I Hope to Leave Behind: The Essential Essays of Eleanor Roosevelt* and *Casting Her Own Shadow: Eleanor Roosevelt and the Shaping of Postwar Liberalism, 1945–1962.*

DENNIS BRACK is a photojournalist who has covered the White House since 1965, most of the time for *Time* and *Newsweek,* averaging a picture a week in each publication for twenty-two years. He has received awards from the National Newspaper Photographers Association, the White House News Photographers Association, and the World Press Association.

WILLIAM B. BUSHONG is historian and webmaster for the White House Historical Association. He received a Ph.D. from George Washington University in 1987. His publications include *North Carolina's Executive Mansion: The First 100 Years* and *Uncle Sam's Architects: The Builders of the Capitol.* He is a regular contributor to *White House History,* the journal of the White House Historical Association.

JOHN ALLEN GABLE is executive director of the Theodore Roosevelt Association and founder of the *Theodore Roosevelt Association Journal,* a quarterly publication with international circulation. He received a Ph.D. from Brown University and is adjunct professor of history at New College, Hofstra University. He publishes, speaks, and appears on television in connection with Theodore Roosevelt and his era.

EDITH B. GELLES is a senior scholar at the Institute for Research on Women and Gender at Stanford University. The Adams presidency, particularly Abigail Adams, has been a major focus of her scholarship. Her publications include *First Thoughts: Life and Letters of Abigail Adams; Abigail Adams: A Writing Life;* and *Portia: The World of Abigail Adams.*

CLIFFORD KRAINIK is an expert on the daguerreotype and early American photography. He mounted an exhibition and produced a catalog on John Plumbe Jr. and his work at the Historical Society of Washington, D.C. With Michele Krainik and Carl Walvoord he is author of *Union Cases: A Collector's Guide to the Art of America's First Plastics.* Both a collector and a conservator of historic photographs, he maintains a studio in Warrenton, Virginia.

MARTHA JOYNT KUMAR served as director of the White House 2001 Project, which was organized to build an institutional memory for seven White House offices in order to provide vital information for new staff. She received a Ph.D. from Columbia University and has published in the *Harvard International Journal of Press / Politics* and *Congressional Quarterly's Guide to the Presidency.* Her book *Wired for Sound and Pictures: The President and White House Communications* is soon to be published.

BETTY C. MONKMAN is curator of the White House. Her gallery exhibitions include "The White House, 1792–1992: Image in Architecture." She was principal consultant for the White House Visitor Center, which opened in 1995. Her *The White House: Its Historic Furnishings and First Families* is a seminal study of White House decorative arts and collections.

WILLIAM SEALE is a historian and editor of *White House History.* His books include *The President's House: A History of the White House; The White House: History of an American Idea;* and *The White House Garden.* Those on other subjects include *Temples of Democracy: The State Capitols of the U.S.A.* and *The Tasteful Interlude.*

RICHARD NORTON SMITH, a historian, biographer, lecturer, and former director of several presidential libraries, is director of the Robert J. Dole Institute of Politics at the University of Kansas. His books include *Thomas E. Dewey and His Times; An Uncommon Man: A Biography of Herbert Hoover; The Harvard Century;* and *Patriarch: George Washington and the American Nation.* He is a frequent television guest, offering commentary on the subjects of the presidency and American history generally.

LYDIA BARKER TEDERICK is assistant curator of the White House. She lectures and publishes on the history of the White House and its collections. Recent articles include "Patriotic Imagery in the White House, 1846–1869" and "A Glimpse of Calvin Coolidge's White House: The Photographs of Ralph Waldo Magee." She has a special interest in photographic documentation of the interior of the White House.

Like No Other House

WILLIAM SEALE

IN the two hundred years the presidents of the United States have occupied the White House, the character of the office can be fairly well divided into parts by century. The presidency envisioned by the Constitution began with George Washington as the powerful head of a world-class state, in the European mold. Thomas Jefferson, elected in 1800, set the tone for a more inward-looking nineteenth century. The office came to be called "chief executive," its limitations implied in the very words.

At the end of the nineteenth century, with international commitments that resulted from the Spanish-American War, the presidency rose to the level of power that the Framers of the Constitution and Washington seemed to have wanted. This took place under William McKinley and was dramatized by Theodore Roosevelt in the new century. "Chief executive" passed into history. Like most great changes, those only seemed sudden. Each had its telling prelude and context, and a thoughtful observer could see them coming.

The White House has served through it all. In the early period, it was the curious big place where the president lived and worked, vastly bigger than most houses and very old-fashioned, even peculiar, in its design. Through time, to most eyes it never changed, and it eventually was to be loved by the American people for this timelessness.

The White House compares easily with no other house—better perhaps to a palace, but the similarities there, even while amusing, are mostly meaningless. A palace today is more likely to be a museum than the home of a head of state. The White House is unique. Once the largest house in the nation, today it seems rather small for the role it plays. An amazing variety of characters has lived there—presidents, of course, but also first ladies and first children. The presidency, beginning as it did near the end of the age of great kings, only a few months before the fall of the Bastille, has a certain footing in the world of crowns and scepters. What else but

For all its two hundred years the White House has been a thoroughfare for great crowds eager to see the president. Seen here on April 4, 1929, it receives thousands at a public reception hosted by the new president, Herbert Hoover.

a king, in the 1780s, was there to base the office of a head of state upon? He was elected, of course, but so were some kings. Stately ceremony surrounded the first two presidents. George Washington, at his weekly receptions, kept one hand securely gripped on the handle of his dress sword and the other occupied with a false-front feathered hat, to discourage the familiarity of handshaking. John Adams, at the White House, received in a black velvet suit just like Washington's, with sword, and stood beneath the Gilbert Stuart portrait of the first president, greeting gentlemen arranged in lines, just as he had seen King George III do in England.

Jefferson threw all of that out. But the whiff of kingliness was not to leave the halls of the White House so easily. Redefined, it was and still is there. Guests thrilled to the dramatic entrance of Andrew Jackson into the East Room, his full cloak flowing, his tall form sweeping beneath an arch crowned with more than a hundred gilt stars pasted on the wallpaper above. The less regal James K. Polk could not provide such physical thunder, but the Marine Band helped by striking up "Hail to the Chief." Everyone turned and looked. For people to look is important to any president. About 130 years later, President Carter ordered the tune to storage, only to bring it out again, for a reason similar to Polk's.

The public loves ceremony at the White House. By the time Jefferson left office, Adams's levees in what is now the State Dining Room were looked back upon nostalgically. James Madison gave Dolley Madison full rein to ignite social fireworks, brightening with good times the lofty rooms the bookish Jefferson had kept dim. Abraham and Mary Lincoln marched down the stairs to Polk's music. Their guests applauded. Rutherford and Lucy Hayes marched to dinner, then afterward led their guests in another, more vigorous march to music, the idea being to distract palates thirsty for liquor, of which none, in that administration alone, was served. The portrait of Lucy Hayes was in the pose of royalty, Temperance's Queen, a sure match for Stuart's kingly portrait of Washington that hung nearby.

No one ever dazzled more grandly than the first Roosevelt, descending a new Grand Staircase tailored to his entrance ceremony, with bugles, band music, and some thirty guests marching two-by-two behind him. Cartoonists often showed him with a crown. The Grand Staircase is no insignificant property of the presidency. William Howard Taft, feeling that he, a huge man, looked awkward descending it, insisted upon using the elevator, but once on level ground, he marched to its foot as proudly as his predecessors. Harry S. Truman, in rebuilding the White House, 1948–52, gave special attention to redesigning the Grand Staircase to provide a gentle, elegant descent but also a platform for something new: a photo-op.

President John F. Kennedy and reporters in the Oval Office.

A mere decade after Truman completed the remodeling, John F. Kennedy extended the idea by transforming the state rooms into a glamorous background for his presidency, assembling splendid furnishings and revising ceremony to a greater extent than any president since Thedore Roosevelt.

Presidential generations pass by within the same walls. The house itself adjusts and is adjusted, but as it grew older, its own influence began to be felt. Presidents began to shape their public appearances with the help of the White House. A house as old as the White House gains the prestige of time; this house has the additional ingredient of history in its succession of important inhabitants. The mystique of the presidency is intimately mingled with the past of the White House, which has grown rich with living.

John Adams, the first occupant, must have found the President's House—as it was soon called, preferred over the original appellation, "palace"—a strange place indeed. He first saw it in the summer of 1800 when it was a regular Babel of Scots, Irish, Africans, and others, rushing to interior completion. He had often said that he would as soon occupy a row house up near the Capitol, but this trip changed his mind. Inspecting the building, he seemed pleased with the plans—except for nude figures on some of the mantelpieces—and he ordered work to go on. A vegetable garden was to be planted, probably where the north front of the Treasury Building now stands. Apparently the ground was turned up, but Adams was not to be there long enough for the harvest.

The second president moved in exactly on November 1, 1800, the day specified in the Residence Act of 1790, which allowed ten years in which to build the Federal City and its two principal buildings, the President's House and the Capitol. Adams found his house still unfinished. One stair was built; the Grand Staircase and secondary stairs were not up yet, so he threaded a little winding service stair to the second floor, where he tumbled into bed, beginning the long legacy. How enormous the President's House must have seemed to those who had known monumentality only in churches and statehouses. Not one of them compared in scale to this, not even Independence Hall!

Huge transverse halls swept east and west with their soaring chambers alongside. Downstairs the windows were large, thin of mullion, with watery crown glass, while upstairs the windows were low to the floor to allow for the high ceilings below and maintain proper proportions for the building from outside. Doors to the principal rooms were made of reddish polished mahogany—crafted in the upstairs oval room—and inlaid with yellow wood from local holly trees. A solitary worker, who seemed a lonely intruder in such a place, stirred up and fed wood fires in the fireplaces night and day in an effort to dry the plaster. Some walls were covered with wallpaper, which must have also been wet. Not all the upstairs rooms were finished. Downstairs the East Room displayed bare brick walls, entirely devoid of plaster, its twenty-two-foot ceilings seeming a mile high. The roof of slate tiles already leaked.

Doors cut along the south front anticipated a long back piazza with a river view, planned with the original house, probably on the request of the first president, who enjoyed his own at Mount Vernon. It was never to be, but the doors meant to access it are still there today. Adams, who was always indifferent about houses, must in any case have wondered at the great basement with its lines of service rooms, the long kitchen with fireplaces at each end, and the mighty groin

Hillary Rodham Clinton's interest in the history of the White House inspired a redecoration of the Blue Room with many elements based on information gleaned from manuscripts in the National Archives.

vaulting of the Cross Hall, meant to support marble floors above and already built when more economical pine was substituted. A hastily built wooden bridge crossed the perilous sunken areaway on the north, giving access to the front door. Adams, not liking this, moved the front to the back, ordering wooden steps built up to what we now call the Blue Room, which became his entrance.

Abigail Adams soon joined her husband, arriving caravan style, bringing the New England couple who kept house for her and some farm girls from Quincy to serve as helpers. She and the president established the southwest corner room upstairs as the master bedroom, which it has been in nearly every administration since. The adjacent room was the office, where John Adams wrote his "midnight appointments" in the last hours of his presidency.

CLINTON PRESIDENTIAL MATERIALS PROJECT

At a dinner to celebrate the two hundredth anniversary of the White House, President and Mrs. Bill Clinton gathered with former presidents and first ladies in the State Dining Room for a group portrait.

Adams's was a stay of short duration. He moved to the President's House in the heat of a bitter presidential campaign and was there in mid-December when the final tally from South Carolina marked his defeat. There was a story told by Jefferson himself, that when he met Adams in the winter of 1801 the outgoing president snapped, "You've put me out!" Jefferson responded calmly that it was not so at all, that it was the *system* which he, Adams, and not Jefferson, had helped create that had put him out of the presidency.

So great were the emotions surrounding the election of 1800 that the city was tense as March 4 approached, the day of Jefferson's inauguration. Fear of insurrection was fairly universal. Adams decided not to remain for the festivities and announced this in the press several days before. Then he departed before daylight,

In the 1890s and early 1900s, the skilled photographer Frances Benjamin Johnston often turned her camera to White House subjects.

leaving the President's House in that strange limbo it still has in the time between the departure of one president and the arrival of another.

It was the two hundredth anniversary of John Adams's moving into the White House that the White House Historical Association celebrated in November 2000 with a symposium held in Washington. This book contains papers presented at the symposium by invited scholars. It does not pretend to provide a comprehensive history of the White House, but a sampling through the two centuries of personalities and images that reflect the place and periods in its history.

Current interpretation and the focus of scholarship shape the contents of symposia. Women's history inspires articles on Abigail Adams and Dolley Madison. Mary Todd Lincoln and Eleanor Roosevelt are studied in the context of their marriages and what they tried to achieve in the White House. The media's role is explored in terms of White House photographers and television. In the course of these essays we revisit the potent eras—the earliest White House and the burning of the house by the British, the Civil War and the Gilded Age, the Progressive era, and the Great Depression and World War II—as well as today.

Giving visual presence to the essays, short pieces with galleries of illustrations take the story from oil and canvas, pencil and paper, to the earliest daguerreo-types—the White House in the dawn of photography—through late-nineteenth-and early-twentieth-century candid portraiture, right down to the rich, often highly penetrating wealth of twentieth-century news photography, when the White House may well be the most frequently photographed building in the world. Nor has television been overlooked.

A history so long, with a purpose so constant, as that of the White House belongs to few other buildings. History often being commemorated in hundred-year intervals, we paused in the year 2000 when human habitation at the White House reached two hundred, and this book is the result. The anniversary passed with the usual pace of time and claimed its own small corner of history. One hundred years earlier, in 1900, the event was celebrated with a luncheon, given by President William McKinley, at which a grand proposal was unveiled for an enlarged and greatly elaborated White House. The more rational renovations of Theodore Roosevelt took place instead, polishing the house for the new twentieth century and the redefined presidency. At midcentury, President Harry Truman's rebuilding prepared the house for the technological age.

The wheels of change have spun faster since then. Today significant plans are also in the works to adjust the White House to the twenty-first century, its fourth literally, but its third in measurement of hundreds. Primary among the challenges to experts consulted on modern needs for security, office efficiency, traffic, and communications is the issue of public access, which must be preserved. Visiting the White House is often the nearest a citizen will ever actually be to the president. Jefferson opened the White House to the public in the spring of 1801 and encouraged people to come. It has been open since, on a regular basis, providing a sort of physical closeness to the president and his scene not usual with heads of state in the world today. This distant echo of the age of kings, when the presidency was created, when the public swarmed over the public rooms of royal palaces hoping for a glimpse, lives on, a cherished privilege of the American people.

To enter the White House is to sense the immediacy of the past and the momentous present. No visitor can miss the special feel of it, even in a slow-moving crowd of fellow observers. The nation's collective memory flows like a river at the White House. Being there calls up familiar dramas of the nation's past and the remarkable characters who performed them. Richard Nixon, in parting, said that it was "like no other house." The White House is a stage for the workings of the pres-

President and Mrs. George W. Bush bid farewell to President Vicente Fox of Mexico and his wife, Martha Sahagún de Fox, on the North Portico, concluding the formalities of a state dinner.

idency and still a setting for the routines of daily and family life. Through the long course of the nation's development the White House has seen it all, public and private. Though itself enduring many changes, in our minds it prevails as unchanged, as perpetual, as the same place known—as it was being built—to the first George and now to two later Georges, a Barbara and a Laura, to John and the loyal Abigail, to Dolley and "the great little Madison," the irascible Andrew, Father Abraham Who Belongs to the Ages and his troubled Mary, the convivial hero General Grant and Julia, the abstemious Rutherford and Lucy, Teddy and Edith, taciturn Calvin and serene Grace, Franklin and the determined Eleanor, Harry and the very private Bess, Jack and the glittering Jackie, Lyndon and Lady Bird, Richard and Pat, Jimmy and Rosalynn, Ronald and Nancy, and all the rest, ongoing.

THE WHITE HOUSE

Actors and Observers

Chapter 1

Abigail Adams
as First Lady

EDITH B. GELLES

WITH great reluctance Abigail Adams boarded her coach on November 2, 1800, to begin her long journey from Quincy, Massachusetts, to the new capital city on the banks of the Potomac River. "You will forgive me, my dear Sister, that I spared both you and myself the pain of a formal leave, and that I left you without bidding you an adieu," she later wrote to her ailing sister Mary Cranch. "I never was so divided between duty and affection, the desire I had to remain with you, and the necessity I was under to commence a long and tedious journey at this late season of the year." She continued to express the dilemma that had become a thematic undertone in her many years of letter writing. "My Heart was rent with the distrest situation. . . . I could not be with you as I wished."[1] Abigail had begun her journey to the new capital city, as she called it, during the least felicitous season for travel and upon a route that had hardly been staked out.

For many years Abigail had used the metaphor of travel to describe the disconnection she experienced between duty and affection, between the life that she preferred to live at home in Quincy among her family and friends and the life she was duty-bound to perform as a public figure. "My Journey was as pleasant as my thoughts upon what was past and my anticipations of what was to come would permit it to be," she had written, and she borrowed a biblical phrase, "splendid misery," to describe the perceived irony in her situation.[2] "To the great Physician both of body and soul I commited you and yours, and sit out with an anxious mind and heavy Heart," she continued in her letter to Mary, checking her complaints and cheering herself by invoking the religion that sustained her in bad times and in good. She further described the weather—"rainy, but promises to clear up"—and noted that the president, her husband, John Adams, had set out from Philadelphia for Washington on the same day that she had departed from Quincy.[3]

Presidents house, Washington City, Nov. 2. 1800

My dearest friend

We arrived here last night, or rather yesterday at one O Clock and here we dined and slept. The Building is in a State to be habitable. And now we wish for your Company. The Account you give of the melancholly State of our dear Brother Mr Cranch and his family is really distressing and must severely afflict you. I most cordially Sympathise with you and them.

I have seen only Mr Marshall and Mr Stoddert General Wilkinson and the two Commissioners Mr Scott and Mr Thornton.

I Shall Say nothing of public affairs. I am very glad you consented to come on, for you would have been more anxious at Quincy than here, and I, to all my other Solicitudines Mordaces as Horace calls them i.e. "biting Cares" Should have added a great deal on your Account. Besides it is fit and proper that you and I should retire together and not one before the other

President John Adams's celebrated letter to his wife, Abigail, written the day after he first moved into the White House, praying heaven "bestow the best of Blessings on this House." President Franklin D. Roosevelt ordered that part of the text carved into the stone fireplace in the State Dining Room.

276a

Before I end my Letter I pray Heaven to bestow the best of Blessings on this House and all that shall hereafter inhabit it. May none but honest and wise Men ever rule under this roof.

I Shall not attempt a description of it. You will form the best Idea of it from Inspection.

Mr Brisler is very anxious for the arrival of the Man and Women and I am much more so for that of the Ladies. I am with unabated Confidence and affection your

John Adams

Mrs Adams

Abigail traveled a route that had become familiar throughout her years in New York, the first capital city, and then in Philadelphia, as John Adams's career had catapulted him first to the vice presidency and most recently to the top office of the land. Now, in the late fall of 1800, John Adams was grappling with his declining political fortunes, as the behind-the-scene machinations of the previous six months had spelled out his forthcoming defeat for a second term. Ever a party to her husband's political struggles, Abigail followed the prescriptions of duty, fighting against the deepest fiber of her own desires, to be by his side in inaugurating the new presidential "castle" in the infant city that was growing out of the marshlands of the Potomac.[4]

In New York City, Abigail passed several grievous days by the bedside of her middle son, Charles, dying, she understood, from the effects of his alcoholism: "At New York I found my poor unhappy son, for so I must still call him, laid upon a Bed of sickness, destitute of a home. The kindness of a friend afforded him an assylum. A distressing cough, an affection of the liver and a dropsy will soon terminate a Life, which might have been made valuable to himself and others. . . . his Physician says, he is past recovery."[5] Continuing her journey, Abigail stayed with her third son, Thomas, now set up in business in Philadelphia, before proceeding into the literally unknown route to Washington.

The conditions of travel did not improve, nor did the weather. After leaving Baltimore at dawn, hoping to make the thirty-six-mile journey to an inn at the outskirts of the new Federal City, her retinue became lost in the woods. "You find nothing but a Forest & woods on the way, for 16 or 18 miles not a village. Here and there a thatched cottage without a single pane of glass," she wrote, ever recording her travelogues to the folks at home to whom such a journey was an unfathomable distance, as we might view travel to some distant planet. She had been invited, she explained, to spend the night with acquaintances along the way, but resisted the imposition. "I who have never been accustomed to quarter myself and servants upon private houses, could not think of it, particularly as I expected the chariot & five more Horses with two servants to meet me." After two long hours of wandering aimlessly through the forest, "holding down and breaking bows of trees which we could not pass," they met a prominent farmer of the area, who guided them back to the path. Within the next hour, the same farmer caught up with her, and she happily accepted from his family private hospitality of the sort that she had formerly resisted. And, she reassured her sister, "I need not add that they are all true federal Characters,"[6] affirming her host's political correctness.

Abigail's reception at Washington was no less felicitous. John Adams met her party and escorted her into the city. "As I expected to find it a new country, with Houses scattered over a space of ten miles, and trees & stumps in plenty with, a castle of a House—so I found it," she remarked, affirming that her expectations had been met. Nor was she disappointed: "The Presidents House is in a beautiful situation in front of which is the Potomac with a view of Alexandria. The country around is romantic but a wild, a wilderness at present."[7] But to her daughter she confided that two issues plagued her. One was bells: in a house so spread out—it would require thirty servants to care for this operation—there were no bells, no way to make contact from one end or floor to another. But more distressing, she wrote, was the lack of wood. "No arrangement has been made . . . to supply newcomers with fuel." Of promises there had been many. Their steward, John Briesler, had, by begging and borrowing, managed to acquire nine cords of wood, but most of that had been used to dry the plaster newly applied to the walls. It was the same throughout the city, Abigail explained. "Congress poured in, but shiver, shiver."[8]

"You must keep all this to yourself, and, when asked how I like it, say that I write you the situation is beautiful, which is true." Always the diplomat, Abigail was mindful, as well, of the viciousness of the press, ever willing to pick up any morsel of bad news to derogate the president. But she confided to her daughter that "the house is made habitable, but there is not a single apartment finished. . . . We have not the least fence, yard, or other convenience, without, and the great unfinished audience-room I make a drying-room of, to hang up the clothes in. The principal stairs are not up, and will not be this winter." She went on to describe inconvenience heaped upon inconvenience and concluded, chauvinistically, that in twelve years of planning and building, New Englanders would have completed the job.[9]

Nevertheless, and despite the inadequacy of the house and its furnishings, Abigail was obliged to entertain. "The ladies are impatient for a drawing room; I have no looking-glasses . . . nor a twentieth part lamps enough to light it. Many things were stolen, many more broken, by the removal; amongst the number, my tea china is more than half missing." The first lady's role allowed no slack for impediments. "You can scarce believe that here in this wilderness city, I should find my time so occupied as it is. My visitors, some of them, come three and four miles. The return of one of them is the work of one day; most of the ladies reside in Georgetown," a village she gave no high marks—"the very dirtiest Hole I ever saw for a place of any trade . . . a quagmire after every rain." Abigail's litany of miseries went on and on—the distances of the markets; the inconvenience that her clothes and furnishings from Quincy, shipped by water, had not arrived; the worry that little Susan, Charles's daughter whom she had brought with her from New York, had "hooping cough, and always the chill and the dampness."[10] All of this splendid misery, however, took place as the backdrop to the real, the meaningful drama of her life that inexorably persisted on two fronts: the seething political fortunes that unraveled as the young and inexperienced nation faced its first, most contested political rivalry for the presidency; and the tragedy that John Adams later called "the greatest grief of my heart and the deepest affliction of my Life,"[11] the death of Charles Adams at the age of thirty-two. To understand all of this, we must pause in our story to look backward in time.

Abigail Adams was the most significant, the most influential, the most important first lady until well into the twentieth century. She gave definition to the role; she came to stand for its nobility; she highlighted its potential. This is true for several reasons. To begin, Abigail Adams was the first occupant of that role who gave independent shape to its parameters. Before her, Martha Washington, a dignified and charming first lady, was totally overshadowed by the towering figure of her husband—as were most members of his administration.[12] Second, Abigail left a paper trail: she wrote letters from which we know quite intimately the dimensions of her participation in the administration of her husband. Third—and to put it plainly—she had and used power.

PLATE 2

The role of first lady is not defined in the Constitution or in any of the laws of the land, and it never has been. The office derives from what the political theorist Carole Pateman calls "the sexual contract." Governments are formed by social contracts made among men, Pateman argues. Men came together and formed a nation and established its guidelines, but nowhere along the line did they make room for the participation of women as citizens. The roles women have exercised for most of history came not from the social contracts, founded among men, but from the marriage contract.[13] Because she was married to the president of the United States, Abigail Adams became first lady—a term, incidentally, that did not come into use until after the mid-nineteenth century.[14] She became a public servant of the state, albeit an unofficial one, because she was Mrs. Adams. That she used that role and how she expanded that role to its very limits were unique to her character, to the character of John Adams, and to the times in which she served.

Abigail did not show up willingly in Philadelphia in April 1797, several weeks after John's inauguration as president, which she skipped. Left to her own devices, she would have remained at home in Quincy, taking care of her manifold responsibilities to family and farm until the fall; and John had concurred with that plan—until he discovered what it meant to sit in the highest office of the new nation.

The High Street House in Philadelphia, one of the city's finest, was rented by the government for George Washington and later John Adams, who left it to move with the government to Washington.

Then, with unremitting urgency, he sent letter after plaintive letter to Abigail, imploring her to join him. "I pray you to come on immediately. I will not live in this State of Separation. Leave the Place to Jonathan & Polly. to Mears—to my Brother—to anybody or nobody. I care nothing about it—But you I must and will have." He pressed his case every few days. "You must come and leave the Place to the mercy of the Winds." And again, "I must now repeat this with heat and earnestness. I can do nothing without you. . . . I must entreat you to loose not a moment time in preparing to come."[15] John had discovered the loneliness of the presidency.

But this was not all. When they were together—and even apart through correspondence—Abigail was his confidante, probably his only lifelong confidante. The role of confidante is specialized; it is rare; it involves a voluntary bond; it is intimate; it has several components. A confidante is a person to whom one can bare one's soul without fear of awful judgment. She is a person who will keep your secrets. A confidante is someone you can trust to be on your side in adversity as well as good times. She is someone with whom you can try out ideas, be creative, even fail, and still trust to be available when you want to try again. She is the person who stands with you when others about you appear suspect, pernicious, mendacious, devious, meretricious, corrupt. In Abigail, John Adams had a confidante. But beside that, Abigail was smart, she was erudite, she was a keen observer of politics, and she generally agreed with John Adams.

PLATE 1

And that takes us to politics in the new republic, which, from the Adamses' point of view, quickly assumed suspect, pernicious, mendacious, devious, meretricious, and corrupt proportions. John Adams, early in his administration, was confronted with problems that had not been predicted or chosen by himself or his administration. The most immediate issues that faced him as president turned on foreign policy. If George Washington had left office warning the nation not to get involved in European affairs, John Adams soon found himself beset by Europe's troubles. The French Revolution and then the Napoleonic Wars threatened to spill into the Western Hemisphere, making it unclear who in Europe was a friend and who was an enemy, and Americans were divided in their loyalties. Shipping was disrupted; seamen were impressed. Invasions were speculated from the North, from the South, from the West. Aliens became suspect.[16] And to complement this full deck of troubles, the media had begun to exercise their power as the fourth estate, becoming, as one early American historian has termed it, the "most violent and vituperative" press in our history.[17]

The crises and the traumas of Adams's administration have been amply recorded.[18] In brief, to his credit, John Adams settled his most gargantuan dilemmas diplomatically; he maintained the dignity of his government and staved off war, but he did so at great cost within his administration. His vice president, Thomas Jefferson, a French partisan at the very least, quickly packed his bags and returned to Monticello. Others were less kind. They remained *in situ* and worked behind the scenes to undermine the efforts of the president. By the last year of his administration, Adams could trust no cabinet member, few congressmen, even from his own state, and few of his own diplomatic appointees. He maintained his policies, and he served his government with integrity, if not tact, with stubborn consistency and political firmness. The one person who traveled this lonely path with him was Abigail. She was the one person with whom he could speak, with whom he could try ideas, with whom he could confess his indecisiveness and his insecurities. Like no other person, she understood, and she could respond with understanding and with wisdom and with political astuteness. We know this because she wrote highly sensitive information in her letters to her sister, to her son John Quincy, minister at Berlin, to Thomas, and to some few others.

"We have letters from Mr. Murray," Abigail wrote to Mary Cranch in January 1798, using the first-person plural and referring to William Vans Murray, American minister to The Hague. "A few lines from Mr. Marshall to him informs him: that the envoys were not received and he did not believe they would be. They dare not write, knowing that every word would be inspected."[19] Abigail's use of the plural was not accidental, though it was possibly unconscious. She was reporting in advance of letters from the recently dispatched envoys that the French Directory had refused to see them. When at last in March news did arrive from the envoys themselves, Abigail informed Mary: "You will learn that at length dispatches have arrived from our commissioners, but with them, no prospect of success. . . . We shall see how the American pulse beat. I fear we shall be driven to War, but to *defend* ourselves is our duty. War the French have made upon us a long time."[20] Again Abigail used the plural, and again she was sending information in advance of public notice. One week later she reported: "I cannot say what Congress mean to do. The dispatches are but just deciphered." She referred to a diplomatic letter, much of which came in code. "Whether the President will think proper to make any further communications is more than he himself can yet determine,"[21] she continued, revealing to Mary that the president was considering his next diplomatic move.

Abigail clearly possessed information about the most recent diplomatic developments as well as her husband's state of mind with regard to those events. She knew in advance of their letters that the American envoys had been rejected by the Directory, that John had not yet decided upon an American response to this dilemma, and that he was studying his options before making a public declaration. Presumably she knew these things because she and he discussed them. The point is that Abigail was unusually well informed—and opinionated—about issues of state that were not yet public information.

If behind the scenes Abigail Adams served as a minister without portfolio and became, in effect, John Adams's shadow cabinet, did he, then, come to depend upon her in making his decisions? Did he lose his way in the morass of politics and intrigue and need the guidance of another person to steer him through these difficult times? Not at all. Nothing about John Adams's performance or behavior during this period suggests that he was anything other than steadfast and decisive. But alone as his own person, he needed a confidante—someone trusted with whom he could try out ideas, think out loud, and make the difficult decisions that come from the weighing of no good options. Abigail served that role; she fit into the interstices of his decision making, and with loyalty—for she always was partisan to his policies—and perspicacity, she helped him to think.

Abigail was further influential in making some appointments in Adams's administration, not only because she knew of appropriate people but also because some people, for whatever reason, went through her to reach the president, as did a longtime family friend, Charles Storer.[22] She developed a strong antipathy for the press and did her best to plant stories that favored her husband (and her son) in a climate of calumny and vituperation. In the end, she strongly favored the passage of a sedition act, advocating it for the states as well as the national government.[23] She served as an informant to her son when other diplomatic sources were not available, so that John Quincy, four to six months distant in communications, was kept more or less abreast of activities in Philadelphia and then in Washington.[24] And finally—no small part of her public office—she was the arbiter of the social scene. Abigail entertained with one large dinner every week and with an open drawing room on afternoons. She repaid obligatory visits. She staged a Fourth of July entertainment for the entire city of Philadelphia each year, and she attended public events that called for her presence. She did this willingly, warmly, and with grace. She set the fashion in attire, modest but of good quality, and in food service. And she did this on the tiny budget permitted by her husband's small salary and the paltry allowance from Congress.[25]

PLATE 3

Now, after three tedious years of his presidency, John Adams was being maneuvered out of office. Abigail watched this happen at first with surprised fascination, then with cynicism and anger that turned to pride and dignity, always reinforced by her religious belief in Providence. She reminded her family time and again that "not a sparrow falls to the ground" without a divine plan.[26]

On November 16, 1800, Abigail arrived in Washington with a heavy heart and began to make the best of an uncomfortable living situation. "Neither my habits, nor my education or inclinations, have led me to an expensive style of living, so that on that score I have little to mourn over," she wrote to Thomas.[27] She was determined to participate in the final scenes of the Adams administration with the same posture of noble sacrifice that had governed her lifetime of patriotic service. She had come because she knew how much John Adams needed her as his companion, but also because her own sense of duty obliged her to be present in the office of first lady. She had left a critically ill favorite sister at home; she was separated from a greatly beloved and dying son; her health was poor—she suffered, among other things, from chronic rheumatism—and she felt her age of fifty-six years.[28] If she sensed that she had little control over circumstances, she sustained strength primarily from her religious faith that assured her a divine plan existed in the mystery of transient life.

Two weeks later, Abigail received the news of Charles's death. "I know, my much loved Sister, that you will mingle in my sorrow, and weep with me over the Grave of a poor unhappy child who cannot now add an other pang to those which have pierced my Heart for several years past," she wrote to Mary.

> Cut off in the midst of his days, his years are numbered and finished; I hope my supplications to heaven for him, that he might find mercy from his maker, may not have been in vain. His constitution was so shaken, that his disease was rapid, and through the last period of his Life dreadfully painful and distressing; He bore with patience & submission his sufferings and heard the prayers for him with composure; His mind at times was much deranged through his sufferings, and through a total want of rest; He finally expired without a groan on Sunday week.

Abigail poured out her grief to Mary. "I was satisfied I had seen him for the last time when I left him. . . . He was beloved in spite of his Errors, and all spoke with grief and sorrow for his habits."[29] Abigail wrote to Mary—and also to her daughter—because she suffered this painful loss of a son in isolation. Even had John Adams, in the midst of his most desperate political battles, been able to shift his focus from government to private life—and perhaps he did and we don't know it—John had rejected his son. Traveling from Quincy to Philadelphia in the fall of 1800 on his return to the then capital city, he passed through New York without stopping to see Charles. "His father has Renounced him, but I will not," Abigail had written John Quincy.[30]

Charles is the mysterious child of the Adams brood. Strangely, few references and almost no correspondence from him survive. What is known of Charles is his reputation as a charming child. He was not noted as brilliant or studious like John Quincy, but rather as attractive because of his sweetness and, perhaps, sensitivity. Born in 1770, Charles was a boy of four when his father left home to serve in the Continental Congress; he knew his father mostly as a revolutionary hero. Then, in 1779, when John Adams returned to Europe on his second diplomatic mission, he took with him not only John Quincy, who had previously accompanied his father in 1777, but also Charles. John Quincy thrived, but Charles was homesick. He was so homesick that his father decided he should return to Quincy, and Charles set off, under the care of a family friend, Benjamin Waterhouse, on the long ocean voyage. Unfortunately, the vessel carrying the child and his guardian went off course and was shipwrecked off the coast of Portugal. For three months Charles languished in Portugal until the repaired ship was ready to continue its voyage.

Charles eventually attended the boarding school run by his affectionate aunt and uncle, who trained him for entrance to Harvard. Afterward, Charles set up a law practice in New York, where he married and had two daughters. When John Quincy departed for Europe in 1794, on the series of diplomatic missions that would keep him abroad for more than a decade, he appointed Charles as overseer of his financial accounts. Whether by inadvertent poor judgment or because the financial markets suffered severe recessions during that period of recovery from one war and threat of another, John Quincy's small fortunes were lost in the stock market. No one, it seems, blamed Charles, but he became distraught.[31] In addition, in the depressed economic climate, it is not clear that he was able to earn a sufficient income to support his own family. Whatever the reasons, Charles's fortunes declined, and he sank into alcoholism. Just as this disease is not fully understood in our own time, it certainly had no scientific or medical basis in the late eighteenth century. Alcoholism represented weakness, if not sin.

But not to Abigail. "He did not look like an intemperate Man—He was bloated, but not red," she confided to Mary in her grief. "He was no mans enemy but his own." She stressed his lovability and signed her letter with an unaccustomed "your afflicted sister."[32] Abigail grieved, and this heavy burden of pain stayed with her, however suppressed and disguised, for the remainder of her three months in the White House.

The election of 1800 was the overriding political drama during the Adamses' last months in office. Despite the consuming emotional drain of her family affairs and the attention she devoted to her public social role, Abigail was keenly involved in the election process, not only because John Adams's (and her own) future was at stake, but because she worried about the survival of the republic. She expressed her concerns to John Quincy in the summer prior to the election, warning him that "it is very difficult for me to give you a clue to the present political agitation without bringing before your view Characters which we have considered as the most respectable in this state. so changed in their sentiments, and in their conduct as to create astonishment." Never a partisan of Alexander Hamilton, whom she variously referred to as "the little cock sparrow" or, for short, just "sparrow," she now coded him as "a certain Little General" who was "possessed of as much ambition of talents. no hopes of becoming commander in chief but by intriguing and bringing in at the approaching election a person who should hold the reigns while he conducted the vehicle."Thus she described the duplicity of Hamilton's injection of Charles Cotesworth Pinckney's candidacy to stir dissension among the Federalists. "Hamiltons language here was that the president had made himself so unpopular by the mission to France, that there was no chance of his being reelected. and therefore . . . Mr. pinckiny was the man who ought to be elected." Another trick, she pointed out, was to represent the "president as Superannuated; true he was to be respected for former services. but now he was grown old and incapable of conducting the government." She added that lies and falsehoods of all sorts had been circulated, and she went on to name names: Cabot, Ames, Higginson and "the Chief Justice," Oliver Ellsworth.[33]

The Adamses' concern for the survival of the new constitutional experiment represented more than their personal interests. Many times after the Washington years, Abigail had feared for the future of the young nation. It must have been a topic in family discussions, for Thomas wrote quite explicitly to his mother—as if continuing one of their personal talks—that "I do not scruple to declare that I think the present Constitution & laws of this Country, so inadequate to the purpose of Government, that I am ashamed to appear as a writer in support of it." Thomas was, in that summer of 1800, observing the machinations that unfolded in Philadelphia as the parties formed into one faction and another. "What is there in such a Government to attach people to it—to create and sustain a wish for its duration—There is in my mind, nothing but *the fear of something worse,*" he underscored the weakness of the system. "Does it hold up anything to gratify any of the predominant passion of the human Heart? Has it any adequate reward for those who embark in its service? Does it afford that protection to property and reputation, which those who submit to it have a right to expect?" With the equation of property and reputation as governmental functions, Thomas conceded that he could go on, but having made his point, he concluded: "I believe, that the people of this Country have but little affection for this Government of their own choice, and yet it has lasted a considerable time by the help of an artificial enthusiasm & a virtuous and wise administration of it." Finally, he warned, "but we are getting unsettled in our opinions wild in our theories and the next change, from present appearances will be for the worse." Thomas did indeed go on, castigating the original enemies of the Constitution—the Livingstons, the Clintons, Aaron Burr, and all the Virginia tribe as well as "small folk here and there."[34]

Thomas's diatribe went to the extreme, even among the Adamses, but Thomas was in Philadelphia. He observed as his father's enemies connived and colluded; he felt the betrayal; and he seems to have inherited some of his father's irreverent rhetorical style. Thomas, too, was passionate. Before signing off with affection to his mother, he added: "But the Old Cat is watching with all her eyes, to seize on a favorable moment of disorder and confusion among the young litter, to make another effort to regain what the old rats some years since stole away from her."[35] Thomas, too, had his favorite labels for Hamilton.

Returns from the November election, finally official in mid-December, eliminated Adams but produced a tie between Jefferson and Burr in the electoral college. During the weeks and months that followed, Abigail and John observed as ballot after ballot was cast in the House of Representatives to determine the next president. "What a lesson upon Elective Governments have we in our young Republic of 12 years old?" Abigail noted to her sister. "What is the difference of Character between a Prince of Wales & a Burr? Have we any claim to the favour of protection of Providence, when we have against warning admonition. . . . Chose as our chief Majestrate a man who makes no pretensions to the belief of an all wise and supreme Governour of the World?" Abigail had always believed and written that a good governor had to be a man of faith. She was, after all, an eighteenth-century New England matron descended from Puritans who had mellowed to Unitarianism—except that in times of crises she sounded once more the old Calvinist creed. "Such are the Men whom we are like to have as our Rulers. Whether they are given us in wrath to punish us for our sins and transgressions, the Events will disclose—But if ever we saw a day of darkness, I fear this is one which will be visible until kindled into flame's."[36] Abigail was not optimistic.

Temperamentally, however, Abigail was not a depressive or a pessimist. She had her moments of dismay—and this was one of them—but she had the capacity to bounce back. She began to look to the future. "The President has enjoyed very good health ever since he has been here, and hopes to be a good Farmer yet," she disclosed to Mary. "He some times says he would go to the Bar again if he had the powers of speech, but of public life he takes a final farewell." She reserved her strongest benediction for her country: "I wish for the preservation of the Government, and a wise administration of it," and she predicted: "In the best situation, with the wisest head and the firmest Heart, it will be surrounded with perplexities, dangers and troubles, that are little conceived of by those into whose hand it is like to fall." She confirmed her intention to serve well to the end of her term of office "and Retire with that dignity which is unconscious of doing or wishing ill to any, with a temper disposed to forgive injuries, as I would myself hope to be forgiven, if any I have committed."[37]

For twenty-five years Abigail Adams had participated in the building of a new nation. As a young wife she had observed the growing tensions with Great Britain; as a young mother she had cared for family and hearth single-handedly, while her husband served his country in Congress; as wife of the first American minister to the Court of St. James's she had presided with dignity in a hostile social and political environment; and finally, following in the footsteps of Martha Washington, whom she greatly admired and wished to emulate as first lady, she rose to new heights in shaping the contours of a public office that no one after her would achieve in just the same manner. She was a singular patriot and a singular servant of her government. She did it all within the framework of an open-ended marriage contract that predicated wifehood and motherhood as its most worthy achievements. But nowhere had it been suggested, when she married John Adams in October 1764, that Abigail would be the first woman to preside over the White House.

As she prepared to leave Washington in early February 1801, Abigail faced another challenge, a familiar one—the difficult and arduous trek home. "I hope I shall be able to encounter this dreadful journey, but it is very formidable to me, not only upon account of the Roads, but the Runs of water which have not any Bridges over them, and must be forded." But first she supervised her last state dinner for the all the judges and other heads of departments and their ladies.[38]

NOTES

1. Abigail Adams to Mary Cranch, November 2, 1800, *New Letters of Abigail Adams, 1788–1801,* ed. Stewart Mitchell (Westport, Conn.: Greenwood Press, 1947), 254.

2. Abigail Adams to Abigail Adams Smith, May 16, 1797, ibid., 89. Thomas Jefferson used the same phrase three days earlier in a letter to Elbridge Gerry, May 13, 1797, Jefferson Papers, Massachusetts Historical Society.

3. Abigail Adams to Mary Cranch, November 2, 1800, *New Letters of Abigail Adams,* 254. Abigail was mistaken. Adams arrived at the White House on November 1, 1800.

4. William Seale, *The President's House: A History* (Washington, D.C.: White House Historical Association, 1986), 83. Seale points out that Abigail called the White House the "castle."

5. Abigail Adams to Mary Cranch, November 10, 1800, *New Letters of Abigail Adams,* 255.

6. Abigail Adams to Mary Cranch, November 21, 1800, ibid., 257.

7. Abigail Adams to Abigail Adams Smith, November 21, 1800, ibid.

8. Abigail Adams to Abigail Adams Smith, November 21, 27, 1800, *Letters of Mrs. Adams, the Wife of John Adams,* ed. Charles Francis Adams (Boston: C. C. Little and J. Brown, 1840), 2:241, 243.

9. Abigail Adams to Abigail Adams Smith, November 21, 1800, ibid., 241–42. Abigail was wrong in her claim of twelve years, for the Residence Act that established the new capital city and its buildings was passed by Congress in 1790. See Seale, *President's House,* 2.

10. Abigail Adams to Abigail Adams Smith, November 21, 1800, *New Letters of Abigail Adams*, 257; Abigail Adams to "dear sister," November 27, 1800, *Letters of Mrs. Adams*, 244.

11. John Adams to Thomas Jefferson, March 24, 1801, *The Adams-Jefferson Letters*, ed. Lester J. Cappon (Chapel Hill: University of North Carolina Press, for the Institute of Early American History and Culture, 1959), 264. Adams wrote this letter soon after the inauguration he so famously avoided by leaving town before daybreak. The longer quotation is "Had you read the papers inclosed they might have given you a moment of Melancholy or at least of Sympathy with a mourning Father. They relate wholly to the Funeral of a Son who was once the delight of my Eyes and a darling of my heart." Perhaps John was trying to offer one explanation for his early departure from the capital.

12. For Martha Washington, see Edith B. Gelles, *First Thoughts: Life and Letters of Abigail Adams* (New York: Twayne Publishers, 1998); Joseph E. Fields, *Worthy Partner: The Papers of Martha Washington* (Westport, Conn.: Greenwood Press, 1994).

13. Carole Pateman, *The Sexual Contract* (Stanford, Calif.: Stanford University Press, 1988).

14. During the Washington and Adams administrations there was no clear form of address for the president or his wife. "First lady" appears infrequently in literature until the twentieth century and did not appear in Webster's *New International Dictionary* until the second edition (1934). See Betty Boyd Caroli, *First Ladies* (New York: Oxford University Press, 1995), xv–xvi, 361–62 n. 7; Fields, *Worthy Partner*, xxv. Since I need to call Abigail something, I have used the term "first lady" anachronistically.

15. John Adams to Abigail Adams, April 1, 7, 11, 1797, Adams Papers, microfilm edition, Massachusetts Historical Society, Boston, reel 384.

16. Stanley Elkins and Eric McKitrick, *The Age of Federalism: The Early American Republic, 1788–1800* (New York: Oxford University Press, 1993), chap. 14; C. Bradley Thompson, *John Adams and the Spirit of Liberty* (Lawrence: University Press of Kansas, 1998).

17. Page Smith, *John Adams* (Garden City, N.Y.: Doubleday, 1962), 2:977.

18. Gelles, *First Thoughts*, chap. 7; Edith B. Gelles, "The Paradox of High Station: Abigail Adams as First Lady," *White House History* 7 (Spring 2000): 4–13.

19. Abigail Adams to Mary Cranch, January 20, 1798, *New Letters of Abigail Adams*, 125.

20. Abigail Adams to Mary Cranch, March 5, 1798, ibid., 140–41.

21. Abigail Adams to Mary Cranch, March 13, 1798, ibid., 143.

22. Charles Storer to Abigail Adams, July 15, 1797, Adams Papers, reel 385. For other examples, see Abigail Adams to Mary Cranch, February 12, 27, 1800, *New Letters of Abigail Adams*, 232–34.

23. Abigail Adams to Mary Cranch, June 19, 23, 1798, *New Letters of Abigail Adams*, 193, 196.

24. George Washington had appointed Adams's twenty-six-year-old son John Quincy as minister to The Hague in 1794; in 1797 his father transferred him to Berlin. See Gelles, *First Thoughts*, 144–47.

25. Unlike some other Founding Families, the Adamses were not wealthy and had few resources to fall back upon during their many years of public service. Since Abigail had taken over responsibility as family financial manager, she fretted constantly about making ends meet. See Edith B. Gelles, *Portia: The World of Abigail Adams* (Bloomington: Indiana University Press, 1992), chap. 3.

26. See, for instance, Abigail Adams to Caroline Smith, February 2, 1809, *Journal and Correspondence of Miss Adams, Daughter of John Adams, Second President of the United States: Written in France and England, in 1785*, ed. Caroline Smith De Windt (Boston: Wiely and Putnam, 1841), 214.

27. Abigail Adams to Thomas Adams, March 10, 1794, *Letters of Mrs. Adams*, 328.

28. Abigail's health had been especially poor in the last decade. She had remained at home in

Quincy for six of the eight years of John's vice presidency and during the third year of his presidency, primarily because of health.

29. Abigail Adams to Mary Cranch, December 8, 1800, *New Letters of Abigail Adams*, 262.

30. Abigail Adams to John Quincy Adams, September 1, 1800, Adams Papers, reel 398.

31. See Smith, *John Adams,* 2:969–70.

32. Abigail Adams to Mary Cranch, December 8, 1800, *New Letters of Abigail Adams*, 262.

33. Abigail Adams to John Quincy Adams, September 1, 1800, Adams Papers, reel 398.

34. Thomas Adams to Abigail Adams, July 19, 1800, ibid.

35. Ibid.

36. Abigail Adams to Mary Cranch, February 7, 1801, *New Letters of Abigail Adams*, 266.

37. Abigail Adams to Mary Cranch, January 15, 1801, ibid., 264, 263.

38. Abigail Adams to Mary Cranch, February 7, 1801, ibid., 266.

Through all of Dolley Madison's later years she saved and cherished this red velvet ball gown. Madison scholar Conover Hunt believes that Mrs. Madison made this gown from the red velvet curtains Latrobe had hung in the Elliptical Saloon, which she rescued the day the White House was burned. In support of this theory, Hunt points out that the velvet is a heavy upholstery grade, not dress goods.

Dolley Madison
Creates the White House

CATHERINE ALLGOR

To modern Americans, the White House is a strange place. Imbued as we are with our notions of things public and private, a single place that encompasses both the private and public lives of the most powerful leader in the world strikes a dissonant note. Even the division of the White House into East Wing and West Wing seems to acknowledge that "work" and "home" should be as separate as possible. To most of us, the White House is a historical throwback to an earlier time, reminiscent of castles and kings. Since the new United States began in part as a reaction against monarchy, this historic analogy may only increase our puzzlement. Why did our Founders decide to set up their chiefs as kings?

But while the White House in fact began as a "palace," it was not built as more than a big house; official men, especially George Washington and Thomas Jefferson, created it to be something new—the executive mansion of a brand-new form of government, one based not on monarchy but on a republican concept. And in the first decades of the nineteenth century, Dolley Payne Todd Madison,[1] one of the Founders, preconceived the building to be a focal point for a capital city, a political center for a new federal government, and a symbol of nationality for a budding nation.

Dolley and James Madison re-created the President's House by loosely adapting two traditions—the Virginia gentry house and the royal house—to suit their official needs. Wanting to secure the future of both Washington City and the nation, the Madisons shaped a White House that gave symbolic definition to the United States, helping to fulfill its destiny as a powerful democracy and a young nation-state.

In the early 1800s the ruling ideology of the official men and their new government was what their leader Thomas Jefferson called "pure republicanism," a philosophy that had fueled the American Revolution, informed the new Constitution, and would also serve as the blueprint for the capital and federal government. Republicanism was a theory with long roots; at its heart was a fear of the abuses of the absolute power that had plagued Europe for generations. In fact, republicanism decried everything associated with royal courts—titles and kings, hereditary aristocracies, the privileges that incited personal interests, displays of luxury, and the involvement of family members and other "unofficial characters."[2]—in short, anything that smacked of politics.

As it turned out, this antipower, antipolitical theory was too frail a basis for a government. Politics was inevitable, and the new United States needed the centralizing power that republicanism forbade. Royal courts, as hierarchical clusters of power, might have been as corrupt as republican theory warned, but they did provide an ordered structure in which the give-and-take of politics might thrive—where rulers could quickly effect change or retain the status quo. The kingly court model supplied the machinery of politics, and members of the founding generation needed all the help they could get on that score. After all, the Constitution was a *model* of government based on republicanism, but when put into practice it proved a little hazy on the day-to-day workings of such a government.

Royal court ceremony was likewise useful in its visible and palpable assertion of power and status. As the European experience proves, courts have the ability to draw loose confederations of states together as single entities, providing emerging nations with a patina of legitimacy in the eyes of the world and, in the best cases, imparting a feeling to the people that they are being well and properly ruled.

This last function of courts brings us to the unresolved tension in the budding American culture in the eighteenth and nineteenth centuries: The ideological commitment to reject aristocracy and monarchy combined with an attraction for the status and stability such aristocratic markers provided; the new Americans were attracted to aristocratic forms. As Richard Bushman has pointed out, the revolutionary generation had been Western European colonists not too long before. The American Revolution did not wipe out an earlier respect for rank.[3] Symbols of aristocracy supplied the only vocabulary of power the new nation knew, imparting messages of strength and solidity to the outside world and to the citizens under rule. Who needed these symbols more than an upstart people who found themselves with a republican experiment that nobody was quite sure would last? So from the first, the new government unfolded within a culture of denial—one that simultaneously rejected monarchical forms, embracing simplicity and republican virtue, all the while longing for the legitimacy of a monarchy.

Washington City—a grand capital on paper and sited in a pastoral countryside—reflected this dichotomy. The impressive classical designs of the buildings were supposed to carry the message of power, while the government they housed was supposed to embody republican weakness. Thomas Jefferson, the second president to rule from Washington City, answered the government's commitment to republicanism and its need for government structure and power by keeping a firm hand on Congress for eight years, deliberately repressing the growth of institutional structures and alliances that would further cooperation and consensus (from our point of view) or collusion and cabal (from his point of view).

Jefferson saw social forms as both producers and products of corruption. For example, in order to eliminate the power of unofficial women that he had seen and loathed in Paris, Jefferson did away with the large social events—the levees—that had surrounded his two predecessors and, he believed, had attracted such dangerous political players. He deliberately simplified social activities at the President's House, limiting himself to small, tightly controlled dinners.[4]

By 1809, when James and Dolley Payne Todd Madison took up residence in the Executive Mansion, they found themselves saddled with a still-undeveloped capital city, an unruly Congress, a shaky foreign policy, and, from almost everyone's point of view, a doubtful national future. Dolley's challenges included legitimizing her husband's administration and the national capital (for both Americans and outsiders), helping him deal with a fractious Congress and a tense relationship with France and Great Britain, and imparting to the citizenry a sense of "Americanness." The couple truly had to go to housekeeping in a global way, shoring the foundations of the nation's structure while presenting a good face to the neighbors. Being members of the gentry class, they reacted the way they knew how in order to establish their presence on the national landscape: they built a house.

PLATE 4

Of course they already had a house—the President's House or President's Palace, as it had been called when its walls were still rising. But whether from indifference or republican rigor, it had languished under Jefferson. If anyone feared that the Executive Mansion was going to be a Versailles, they had no fear in 1809: it was shabby indeed. Jefferson had taken a great interest in the initial design and building of the mansion, but his attention waned as he focused on other presidential matters. The mansion's location away from the rest of the official buildings of Washington was probably supposed to suggest lofty distance; in 1809, it suggested only isolation. With no levees and a restricted dinner schedule (each congressman was entertained at a meal once a season), Jefferson did not encourage the official and unofficial elite of Washington City to call.

Even before James Madison's inauguration, Dolley Madison made it clear that

PLATE 5

things must change, and she began with the house. In any book on the first ladies, one will find a sentence such as "Dolley Madison redecorated the White House." Modern people think they know what that means: houses are the domain of women, the site of leisure and emotion, in direct contrast to the life outside the home, in public. Today, it seems natural and logical that James Madison turned this house project over to Dolley.

But in the eighteenth and early nineteenth centuries, house building among the elite was more than an expression of a private aesthetic, more than a desire for privacy and comfort. In a world that did not yet radically distinguish public life from private, elite men and women did the business of the day in their houses, often in the context of social events such as dinners, parties, and afternoon calls. Furthermore, houses were often symbolic, proudly dominating the landscape of an area. For families for whom the family business was politics, the house was a man-ifestation of superior status, a concrete signifier of their right to rule. The way a big house looked, then, was more than a matter of personal taste.[5] It is significant that men, like George Washington at Mount Vernon, Thomas Jefferson at Monticello, and many other less-famous men of the ruling classes, concerned themselves with questions of architecture, paint colors, furnishing, and decorative issues. They saw the projection of aesthetics as part of their political mission, a class responsibility, even a reflection of their inner worthiness. So when James entrusted Dolley with the re-creation of the executive mansion, he assigned her a public duty, one crucial to establishing his status and authority.

Dolley didn't let him down. With Capitol architect Benjamin Henry Latrobe, Dolley embarked on a project that was less a redecorating than a *restructuring* of the President's House. Their objective was not to create a comfortable fireside for a weary husband, a private haven in a heartless public world. Rather, in designing a state dining room, a parlor, and a grand drawing room, they produced a *national symbol,* a *ceremonial focus* for the local Washington communities, and a *practical place* for the day-to-day business of politics. Latrobe was obviously in tune with Dolley's larger visions. Six days after the inauguration and before the Madisons had actually moved into the house, he spent $3,150 on what he called "the most *necessary* arti-cles of furniture"—four pairs of mirrors.[6]

Initial plans focused on fashioning large public rooms, suitable both for enter-taining and for establishing an image of material sophistication. Dolley and Latrobe began with two rooms—the small sitting room (now the Red Room, then called "Mrs. Madison's parlor") and the large oval drawing room, today's Blue Room.

The choices of decor and function for these rooms reflected the tension in American culture between aristocratic-monarchical impulses and republican-democratic energies. Rather than trying to subdue this tension, Dolley appropriated all the best parts. She and Latrobe created an elegant suite of rooms, upholstered and draped with rich fabrics, adorned by great mirrors, and lighted by silver wall lamps. The sofas were emblazoned with the shield of the Union, and Dolley and Latrobe included other furniture and decorations with a Greek theme, as befitting a government that involved its citizenry. Dolley distributed nationalistic art and American manufactures throughout.[7]

PLATE 6

The transformation succeeded admirably. Descriptions dating from this time are many and favorable: "The President's house is a perfect palace," exclaimed one visitor. Dolley's genius lay not in her taste but in her ability to combine republican simplicity with federalist high style. The Madisons and Latrobe knew that their audience would be composed in part of European diplomats, accustomed to refinement and convention; a fair number of Federalists, for whom formality and elegance signaled a proper attitude toward tradition and power; and the more democratically minded Americans from across the country, who needed to savor the grandeur of state.[8]

In a culture that responded to symbolism in architecture, the new White House became a focus for visitors of all nationalities and most classes who found their ways to Washington. This period marks the beginning of the identification by the American people with "their" house, which would prove critical in 1814 when the British burned the White House. Galvanized by the atrocity of the act, the American people would rally around their government and their president.

Both the parlor and the oval drawing room constituted some of the most fashionable interiors in nineteenth-century America. They became a stage setting for Dolley's primary mission—to counteract a constitutionally weak presidency by establishing her White House as a practical place for politics. The parlor was finished first, and it functioned as a space for the intricate calling rituals that in other cities helped to build an elite. In Washington, from the first, *everything* had political ramifications, and the calling rounds were no exception. In contrast to how Jefferson used his executive mansion, Washington ladies and gentlemen, foreigners, and travelers felt free to call on Dolley Madison and interacted with each other in her parlor.

But Dolley's greatest triumph lay in the new, opulent drawing room. She adapted the form of the court levee, which she and James dubbed "the drawing room," in the British manner, a seemingly more democratic appellation than the

European "salon." There Dolley also blended the pull of aristocracy with the push of what would become known as "democracy," creating what scholar Holly Cowan Shulman calls "ceremonies suitable for a new republic."[9] Where Martha Dandridge Washington and Abigail Smith Adams created entertainments that linked formal ceremony and exclusive invitations with simple settings and dress, Dolley's solution to the "aristocratic/republican" paradox combined sumptuous settings and regal sartorial choices with an inclusiveness that was downright democratic.

Mrs. Madison's Wednesday night drawing rooms began on March 30, 1809, and lasted to the end of Madison's administration, when the president was in temporary quarters. At some points before and during the War of 1812, the drawing rooms provided the only place where political enemies met and talked civilly. In the beginning, Dolley placed announcements of the drawing rooms in the newspapers as a general invitation. And the people came—sometimes two or three hundred at a time and as many as five hundred during the war years. Sources tell us that Americans of all classes attended. There are tales of drivers of hired hacks who, dropping their fares at the president's house, then parked their horses and came in for a drink themselves.[10]

One outstanding feature of these events was the lack of ceremony. Aside from an initial greeting to the Madisons, guests moved freely about the three receiving rooms, much like a modern cocktail party. Groups gathered, broke up, and reformed throughout the evening. Even the food was on the move, carried through the crowd on large trays by slaves and possibly also servants. As depicted in Margaret Bayard Smith's 1828 novel, *What Is Gentility?,* Dolley's movements often dictated the rhythm of the crowd. Butchers and boardinghouse keepers' daughters, as well as diplomats and refined ladies, trailed after the regal Mrs. Madison, who might be resplendent in, say, a pink satin dress trimmed with ermine and sporting headgear that, to the most republican of the Republicans, looked suspiciously like a crown.[11]

Dolley created a social milieu peculiar to Washington City, one that the travel writer Frances Trollope would later describe as having "so little attention to ceremony . . . [that] it is possible that many things may be permitted there, which would be objected to elsewhere."[12] This power of possibility did very nicely for a political environment of government officials trying to create a working structure, and everyone politicked at the drawing rooms. By inventing these drawing rooms, Dolley constructed a political space unlike any existing in Washington. In contrast to Jefferson's rigidly controlled settings, which allowed for no private conversations, Dolley's soirees encouraged a fluid, freewheeling atmosphere of political activity that could accommodate any numbers and combinations of folks, one that encouraged display and ample private conversation.

Unlike Jefferson's dinners, the "Wednesday nights" included both Republicans and Federalists, cabinet secretaries as well as members of Congress. In addition, the "open house" nature of the event allowed for visitors—government and military officials from all parts of the country—as well as the wives and other male and female kin of government workers. Dolley created the political space, and then she invited everyone to participate.

Access is the key to politics, and access is what Dolley Madison's glamorous White House was all about. Political scientists remind us that access is the first building block toward fashioning a working political culture. Access begins the process of communication and then nurtures the personal relationships that keep the political machine running.[13] At no other time in the history of the executive, before or since, was anyone, resident or visitor, so likely to have the chance for a quiet discussion with the president of the United States. Sources reveal lots of other politicking between and among the diplomatic corps and the cabinet and congressional families at the drawing rooms. These activities included, but were not limited to, obtaining, giving, or disseminating information (especially about the likelihood of war); proposing future legislation or political projects; seeking patronage and office; mediating conflicts and compromises; and "horse-trading" of all kinds.[14]

Dolley accomplished and extended many of her goals and projects with these soirees. She did a great deal of meat-and-potatoes politicking, including practicing patronage, at which she was particularly adept. The staffing of the early federal government reflects her efforts to an amazing extent. But her work also included a category of metapoliticking centered in her role as the charismatic figure of her husband's administration. She used her charisma in two ways: first, to personify the legitimacy and accessibility of power in the new nation, especially during the War of 1812; and second, to help her husband's relationship with what many historians call the worst Congress ever dealt a president.

Congress split violently over the prospect of war with Britain, resulting in massive congressional overturn toward favoring war in the election of 1810. Once President Madison sent a war message to Congress and war was declared, June 19, 1812, the legislators' hostility escalated. Several times the infighting threatened to split the Union, culminating ultimately in the Hartford Convention's unsuccessful bid for secession in 1814–15.

Furthermore, there was no constitutional way for the president to calm an unruly legislature; there were no avenues of control and structure in the government
and no political parties. The president's best strategy lay in statecraft, of which so-
cializing forms an important component.[15] Jefferson was adept at it, and it con-
tributed to his effective leadership. Unfortunately, in that sense, James Madison was
no Thomas Jefferson. But Dolley was.

The secret of Dolley's success lay in her creation of herself as what I call "the
Republican Queen," paradox though it might seem. As Republican Queen, Dolley played on the attractions of aristocracy combined with the ideological commitment to republicanism, not by trying to reconcile or disguise the two conflicting currents but by brazenly laying them out side by side. Much as her social
events combined elegance of setting beyond the imaginings of most Americans
with a freewheeling informality, Dolley mixed her sweet, almost homey, personality with the decorative dress and bearing of a leader.

Dolley had the common touch. This was a woman who possessed, as observers
noted, "the magic power of converting enemies into friends." Another described the
secret of her charm: "You like yourself more when you are with her."[16] At the same
time, Dolley dressed herself in the most gorgeous and extravagant costumes. One
could hardly imagine Martha Washington in ermine, or in Dolley's rose-colored
satin gown with a white velvet train. Even upper-class American women did not
wear accessories such as ostrich plumes or gold chains that clasped around waist and
wrists; nor did they wear emerald earrings in the shape of "M." Observers noted,
with a range of emotions from amusement to adoration to horror, the regal themes
of Dolley's ensembles, especially crown motifs variously described as a silver head-
dress, a *sparkling diadem,* and a white velvet turban trimmed with white ostrich tips
and a gold-embroidered *crown.*[17]

Clothing, however, represents only one element in establishing a charismatic
presence; bearing or mien also solidifies a leader's claim to rule. While praising
Dolley's ensembles, many observers hastened to add that her appeal was not merely
as a conveyor of clothes. As Sarah Gales Seaton, Washington observer, proclaimed,
"'Tis not her form, 'tis not her face, it is the woman altogether, whom I should
wish you to see."[18]

Dolley lived in a culture that quite self-consciously associated personal bearing with a leader's qualifications. The notion that a leader should "look the part"
had a long history in court behavior and survives in many an august royal portrait.
The American Revolution and the new republic shifted this point of view but did
not abandon it.[19] George Washington was more kingly than any king of his time.

Dolley may have been an American and a republican, but it is also clear that she demonstrated an awareness of the function of charisma and conducted herself in a manner worthy of a court lady.

Everyone got the message: the wife of that sober republican James Madison was widely and popularly known as "Queen Dolley." Washington visitors and residents subjected Dolley's conduct, her clothing, and her jewelry to political analysis. Their minute examinations and their subsequent approval testify to the durability and longevity of these courtly ideals. No officials know better the importance of charismatic performance than diplomats and their spouses, and it is significant that most of the diplomats who came to the United States heaped extravagant praise upon Mrs. Madison. A Danish minister who attended many Madison drawing rooms exclaimed: "What need you manners more captivating, more winning, more polished, than those of that amiable woman?" He went on in that vein, concluding, "She moves like a goddess, and she looks a queen."[20]

Appearance is only one element of charisma; character counts, too, or, perhaps more cynically, the appearance of character. Contemporaries and historians have long lauded Dolley for what they call her "good heart," describing her kindness and charm as personal, womanly qualities. But these categorizations obscure Dolley's objective, which was to bind people to her and to her husband, forging the alliances that would solidify her James's administration. She especially focused her political energies on winning over members of Congress.

Dolley has long been famous as a hostess. She is remembered as a woman who seemingly rose above partisan politics to include everyone under her roof. As representative from Pennsylvania, Jonathan Roberts commented approvingly, "by her deportment in her own house, you cannot discover who is her husband's friends or foes."[21] This was an era in which politicians accused each other of heinous acts and in a few cases even murdered one another over words.[21] Yet week after week, Dolley Madison, with a smile and a gracious sally, welcomed men into her home who had publicly pilloried her husband and who had accused her and her beloved younger sister of sleeping with men for votes.

Many "Dolley stories," cited to demonstrate her generous, inclusive "nature," instead show that she foreshadowed a modern attitude toward politics, one that encompassed a two-party system. In an age characterized by "passion," by heated all-or-nothing rhetoric, Dolley's assumption that compromise would be the salvation of the system marks her as one of the most sophisticated politicians of her time. She disguised her emotions, providing enemies with access to her self, her husband, and other legislators and moving easily in a bipartisan milieu of cooperation

WHITE HOUSE COLLECTION

Soot from the burning of the White House still scars the lush carving surrounding the north doorway. White paint covers it now, but not because of the soot. Painting the house white was a custom begun well before the first occupant moved in.

because she was a master politician. Power sharing and compromise—the requisites for an effective democratic political culture—seemed inconceivable to the men in the power structures but not to Dolley, who built coalitions and connections every week in the apparent innocence of her drawing rooms.

Seymour Martin Lipset has demonstrated in his analysis of the origins of American exceptionalism that the role of the charismatic figure goes beyond mere personal efforts. The true measure of a charismatic figure lies in her ability to personify—extending, reflecting, and refracting meaning.[23] From 1809 to 1817, Dolley Madison was very probably the most famous person in the United States. This was never more true than during the dark days of the War of 1812, when she, not her husband, became the figurehead of the war effort.

Always the more conspicuous of the Madison team, Dolley's visibility had increased during the war. The American forces enjoyed few victories, but Dolley made much of military heroes, such as Oliver Hazard Perry and William Henry Harrison, highlighting their achievements and honoring them personally when they came to town. Dolley, not James, spoke to the troops—"presenting them with an elegant standard, accompanied by a patriotic address"—and christened ships at the Navy Yard. When the Americans captured the British warship *Macedonian* in 1813, the crew presented the ship's flag to her during her drawing room. As they spread the British standard at her feet, a rare glimpse of the emotions behind Dolley's public persona emerged; one observer reported, "I saw her color come and go."[24]

As peace came, when the Treaty of Ghent arrived in Washington City, one observer noted of Dolley Madison, "*She* was, in her person . . . the representative of the feelings of him who was, at this moment, in grave consultation with his official advisors." Dolley had taken upon herself the task of providing reassurance and stability. The observer continued: "No one could doubt, who beheld the radiance of joy which lighted up her countenance and diffused its beams around that all uncertainty was at an end and that the government of the country had, in very truth . . . 'passed from gloom to glory.'"[25]

In this case, "Republican Queen" contains as deep a paradox as "Republican Court," since the role encompasses a variety of mutually conflicting tasks. The ideology of republicanism precluded the assertion of authority and legitimacy, as well as the structure- and coalition-building that the still relatively new federal government required to grow and thrive. Through selective borrowing from court culture, the charismatic figure of "the Republican Queen," as invented by Dolley, adapted republicanism for political needs.

Though Dolley Madison and her White House are the most visible manifestations of female political work, white, middling, and elite women in Washington and all across the country were engaged in similar political activities. Dolley and women like her were not feminists; they were the essentially conservative wives, mothers, and daughters of political families, and they saw their work not in terms of their personal power but as furthering their families' interests. They succeeded precisely because they were covered by the veil of gender prescriptions. By using the techniques they knew best—social events, benevolence and charity, and networks of kith and kin—their efforts helped to secure the government, the capital, and the nation.

PLATE 8

Ironically, in Washington women's work also preserved republicanism in its purest form. In a twist on the separate spheres, by taking on the pragmatic work of politics—the "dirty work"—Dolley and her set preserved the appearances of their husbands' philosophical purity. When the democratic surge forced United States politics to change in the 1820s and 1830s, the rudimentary machine that Washington political families had built in the unofficial sphere would ease that transition at the federal level. And the White House, as conceived by James and Dolley Payne Todd Madison, would stand at the center of the first modern democracy and a powerful nation-state—truly a people's palace, a jewel in a democratic crown.

NOTES

1. I should explain my use of first names. Feminist biographies center women as subjects in their own right and are concerned with gender considerations and relationships of power among individuals and within culture. The power of language, specifically the power to name, thus emerges as an explicit issue. I refer to wives and husbands inside political teams by first names; if this practice results in diminution by excessive familiarity in the reader's mind, at least both partners will suffer it equally. Whenever a woman is referred to by full name, some effort is made to acknowledge her natal name and kin markers, for example, "Dolley Payne Todd Madison."

2. Lance Banning, *The Jeffersonian Persuasion: Evolution of a Party Ideology* (Ithaca, N.Y.: Cornell

University Press, 1978), 59, 83, 201. The literature on republicanism and its role in the founding era is extensive, but Banning remains one of the best sources. See also Stanley Elkins and Eric McKitrick, *The Age of Federalism: The Early American Republic, 1788–1800* (New York: Oxford University Press, 1993), 6–21.

3. Richard L. Bushman, *The Refinement of America: Persons, Houses, Cities* (New York: Alfred A. Knopf, 1992), 40.

4. James Sterling Young, *The Washington Community, 1800–1828* (New York: Columbia University Press, 1966), 168, 190–191; Joseph J. Ellis, *American Sphinx: The Character of Thomas Jefferson* (New York: Alfred A. Knopf, 1993), 191; Joanne B. Freeman, "Jefferson and Political Combat" (paper presented at "New Horizons in Jefferson Scholarship," International Center for Jefferson Studies, Charlottesville, Va., October 4–5, 1996). See also Andrew Burstein, *The Inner Jefferson: Portrait of a Grieving Optimist* (Charlottesville: University Press of Virginia, 1993), 223; David S. Shields and Fredrika J. Teute, "Jefferson in Washington: Domesticating Manners in the Republican Court" (paper presented at the Institute of Early American History and Culture, June 7, 1997). For an example of Jefferson on political women, see Thomas Jefferson to George Washington, December 4, 1788, *Papers of Thomas Jefferson,* ed. Julian P. Boyd et al. (Princeton, N.J.: Princeton University Press, 1950–), 14: 330.

5. Bushman, *Refinement of America,* 96–97.

6. Benjamin Henry Latrobe to James Madison, March 10, 1809, James Madison Papers, Library of Congress, Washington, D.C.

7. For a detailed examination of this process, see Conover Hunt-Jones, *Dolley and the "great little Madison"* (Washington, D.C.: American Institute of Architects Foundation, 1977).

8. Holly Cowan Shulman, "Dolley (Payne Todd) Madison," in *American First Ladies: Their Lives and Legacy,* ed. Lewis Gould (New York: Garland Publishing, 1996), 54.

9. Ibid., 56.

10. Elizabeth Ellet, *Court Circles of the Republic* (Hartford, Conn.: Hartford Publishing Company, 1869), 83.

11. Margaret Bayard Smith, *What Is Gentility?* (Washington, D.C.: Pishey Thompson, 1828), 150.

12. Frances Trollope, *Domestic Manners of the Americans* (1832; Barre, Mass.: Imprint Society, 1969), 194–95.

13. David Truman, *The Governmental Process: Political Interest and Public Opinion* (New York: Alfred A. Knopf, 1971), 322, 324.

14. Betty Boyd Caroli, "The First Lady's Changing Role," in *The White House: The First Two Hundred Years,* ed. Frank Freidel and William Pencak (Boston: Northeastern University Press, 1994), 180.

15. Young, *Washington Community,* 157–59.

16. Anthony Morris to Anna Cutts, June 26, 1837, quoted in Grace Dunlop Peter, "Unpublished Letters of Dolly Madison to Anthony Morris Relating to the Nourse Family of the Highlands," *Records of the Columbia Historical Society* 44–45 (1942–43): 217–18.

17. Sarah Gales Seaton, diary, in *William Winston Seaton and the National Intelligencer,* ed. Josephine Seaton (Boston: James R. Osgood, 1871), 113; Margaret Bayard Smith to Susan B. Smith,

March 9, 1809, Margaret Bayard Smith Papers, Library of Congress; Phoebe Morris to Anthony Morris, February 17, 1812, Dolley Madison Collection, Dumbarton House, Washington, D.C.; Margaret Brown Klapthor, *The First Ladies Cookbook* (New York: Parents' Magazine Press, 1969), 47; Harriet Otis, journal, January 1, 1812, Harrison Gray Otis Family Papers, Massachusetts Historical Society, Boston.

18. Sarah Gales Seaton, diary, January 2, 1814, quoted in *William Winston Seaton,* ed. Josephine Seaton, 113.

19. Lester Cohen, "The Politics of Language and the Aesthetics of Self," *American Quarterly* 35 (1983): 481.

20. Quoted in Ethel Stephens Arnett, *Mrs. James Madison: The Incomparable Dolley* (Greensboro, N.C.: Piedmont Press, 1972), 1.

21. Quoted in Linda Grant De Pauw and Conover Hunt, *"Remember the Ladies": Women in America, 1750–1815* (New York: Viking Press, 1976), 149. Some historians have begun to see Dolley this way. Ethel Stephens Arnett was the first modern historian to assert Dolley's importance to political history; however, her use of evidence was not satisfactory. The work of Carl Anthony and Holly Cowan Shulman explicitly concerns issues of political power. Unfortunately, they have not been able to explore the topic more fully, as they have written about Dolley only in the context of short essays in larger first lady collections. See Carl Sferrazza Anthony, *First Ladies: The Saga of the President's Wives and Their Power, 1789–1961* (New York: William Morrow, 1990). In the 1990s, Judith Waldrop Frank appeared as Dolley in lectures and presentations, and also ventured similar thoughts in a personal communication to the author.

22. Joanne B. Freeman, "Dueling as Politics: Reinterpreting the Burr-Hamilton Duel," *William and Mary Quarterly* 53, no. 2 (April 1996): 289–318.

23. Seymour Martin Lipset, *The First New Nation: The United States in Historical and Comparative Perspective* (New York: Basic Books, 1963), 18–22.

24. Anthony, *First Ladies,* 88–89; Irving Brant, *James Madison: Secretary of State* (Indianapolis: Bobbs-Merrill, 1953), 451; Sarah Gales Seaton, diary, January 1, 1813, quoted in *William Winston Seaton,* ed. Josephine Seaton, 91.

25. "Thirty-Four Years Ago: A Reminiscence," undated newspaper clipping (probably *National Intelligencer*), Cutts Collection, Massachusetts Historical Society.

Washington photographer John Plumbe Jr. produced this image of the south front of the White House on an afternoon in early spring during the James Polk administration. Taken in 1846, only five years after the invention of the art itself, it is the first photograph of the White House.

Chapter 3

The Earliest Photographs of the White House, 1840s

CLIFFORD KRAINIK

FROM its construction two hundred years ago, the White House was a favorite venue for artists. Designed and built over a period of eight years in the 1790s, this grand neoclassical structure was sketched and painted with varying degrees of accuracy throughout the early nineteenth century. It was not until 1846, however, with technical advances in photography, that the first unerring likeness of the building was secured. In the early spring of that year the nationally known photographer John Plumbe Jr. embarked on an ambitious project to record the federal buildings in Washington, D.C. His work included photographs of the U.S. Post Office, the Patent Office (now the National Portrait Gallery), a spectacular view of the United States Capitol showing the old wooden dome by Charles Bulfinch, and the first known photograph of the White House.

Plumbe recorded these buildings using the earliest form of photography—the daguerreotype process—and produced unique images on silver-plated sheets of copper. It was a demanding procedure requiring great technical skill; the danger to the operator of chemical poisoning was a constant. Plumbe intended to exhibit the architectural views free to the public in his Pennsylvania Avenue gallery and to sell copies of these splendid photographs. In 1973 the Library of Congress acquired a set of six extremely rare and historically important Plumbe daguerreotypes, including the remarkable first photograph of the White House.

John Plumbe's view of the White House was taken on a sunny afternoon in the early spring, while President James K. Polk and his wife, Sarah Childress Polk, occupied the mansion. The camera was directed toward the north and east. We can establish the year the photograph was taken based on Plumbe's newspaper advertisements; the season is evident by the piles of melting snow at the bottom of the South Portico's circular stairs and the numerous budding trees. The time of day the picture was made can be told from the reflection of the sun in the westward fac-

35

ing side windows and the direction that the shadows fall from the White House pillars. Details in this photograph are exacting. We can discern the fencing that separated the flower and vegetable gardens from the White House lawn. Even the right-angled stovepipes poking up from the White House chimneys are visible. The first photograph of the President's House is an image that provides a wealth of information about the building in general, with its grounds and plantings, and a multitude of details that no drawing or painting could ever convey.

James Knox Polk, a Jacksonian Democrat from Tennessee, was the first "dark horse" candidate to win the presidential office. In the November general election

James K. Polk is dramatically portrayed in this hand-colored lithograph published by Nathaniel Currier in 1846. The New York–based printmaker acknowledged that the portrait was made "from a daguerreo-type by Plumbe." Polk was the first president to be extensively photographed while in office during an era that saw widespread use of the new art.

COLLECTION OF CLIFFORD AND MICHELE KRAINIK

of 1844, Polk captured 50 percent of the popular
vote and 62 percent of the electoral ballots to become, at age forty-nine, the youngest president up to
that time. Described as hardworking, industrious,
and a plodding administrator, Polk had a clear vision
for his presidency. High on his agenda was the acquisition of western lands.

Polk was pursued by photographers even before
he took the oath of office. As early as February 1845
John Plumbe was planning to photograph the new
president with his cabinet. On February 27, 1846,
after slightly less than a year in office, President Polk
dutifully recorded in his diary the occasion of his daguerreotype portrait: "Mr. Shank of Cincinnati,
Ohio, who was taking Daguerreotype likenesses of
the ladies of the family in one of the parlors below
stairs, requested to take mine for his own use, and I
gave him a sitting. He took several good likenesses."[1]
The camera operator, Abel Shank, was employed by
John Plumbe. This is the first recorded instance of
the president of the United States being photographed inside the White House. The very few

*Small "French antique" side chair, one of a large number
purchased by Sarah Polk for the State Dining Room. See
photograph of Polk's cabinet, page 42.*

previous presidential photographs were taken either in the Capitol or in a photographer's studio. The fact that a photographer was admitted into the inner circle of
the president's quarters speaks to the degree of accessibility President Polk afforded
to artists. Although the photographs taken by Shank are not presently located, there
does exist a fine pair of Nathaniel Currier lithographs of the president and the first
lady. Both lithographs are dated 1846 and state in the lower margin that they were
made from daguerreotypes by Plumbe.

Possibly one of the daguerreotypes of President and Mrs. Polk taken at the
White House on February 27, 1846, by Abel Shank is represented by the portrait
in the collection of the James K. Polk Home, Columbia, Tennessee. This likeness
was still among the possessions of Mrs. Polk when she died in 1891. One of the
youngest and most handsome of presidential couples, both were from pioneer
southern families and assumed their official responsibilities with great care. Sarah
Polk banished hard alcohol and dancing from the President's House, limited entertaining to traditional events, and observed the Sabbath rigidly.

Sarah Childress Polk, shown in a lithograph by Nathaniel Currier that was based on an 1846 daguerreotype by John Plumbe Jr. Mrs. Polk loved elegance, indeed richness, and devised the Red Room as red, with carved, French-style furniture. She saw gaslight introduced to the White House. But she banned dancing and ardent spirits from White House social affairs, permitting only wine in deference to the diplomatic community.

With the annexation of Texas, Mexican–American relations were doomed. On May 13, 1846, Congress declared "a state of war" with Mexico as a result of a military engagement between Mexican forces and troops Polk sent to a disputed region. Despite the many demands of the war, President Polk agreed to accommodate the portrait painter George P. A. Healy's request for a likeness. After taxing the president with more than thirteen hours of sittings, Healy made a final request for a daguerreotype session. In his diary entry of June 16, 1846, President Polk recorded, "Mr. Healy, the artist, requested the cabinet & myself to go into the parlor and suf-

James and Sarah Polk, captured about 1846 in this daguerreotype by John Plumbe Jr., were considered a handsome couple; she was often called "the Spanish Donna" for her black hair, flashing eyes, and love of lacy mantillas. They presided over a brilliant wartime White House, although the dour Polk's diary makes his single term sound quite workaday.

JAMES K. POLK MEMORIAL ASSOCIATION, COLUMBIA, TENNESSEE

fer him to take a daguerreotype likeness of the whole of us in a group. We gratified him. We found Mrs. Madison in the parlor with the ladies. Three attempts were made to take the likeness of myself, the Cabinet, & the ladies in a group, all of which failed."[2] Although the president made note of the failed attempts to take group portraits inside the dimly lit White House, a surviving daguerreotype might represent the successful work of the artist-turned-photographer at the same time. Held in the collection of the International Museum of Photography at the George Eastman House, Rochester, New York, this extraordinary daguerreotype portrays President and Mrs. Polk posed with friends and family on the South Portico of the White House.

This photograph brings together five occupants of the White House, past,

On the South Portico Sarah and James K. Polk are surrounded by friends and members of his cabinet, as well as the aged Dolley Madison, always a welcomed dinner guest of the Polks. Mrs. Madison did not hold her pose steadily enough for the long exposure.

current, and future. The lofty windows of the Blue Room serve as an incidental backdrop for people who span twelve presidential administrations, from James Madison's before the War of 1812 to James Buchanan's at the eve of the Civil War. At the far left stands Polk's secretary of state, James Buchanan. Next to him is his niece, Harriet Lane. Eleven years into the future Buchanan would become the fifteenth president of the United States, with Harriet Lane serving as his White House hostess. They would occupy the President's House during the tumultuous years just prior to the Civil War. The young girl next to Harriet Lane is Joanna Rucker, a favorite niece of Mrs. Polk. Towering behind Joanna Rucker is Postmaster General Cave Johnson, best remembered for his introduction of the U.S. postage stamp. Peeking between Mrs. Polk and the president is the secretary of the treasury, Robert Walker, the guiding force behind the Independent Treasury system. The blurred figure to the right of President Polk is the venerable Dolley Madison. The bonneted woman to the right of Mrs. Madison is Matilda Childress Catron, Mrs. Polk's first cousin.

John Plumbe's desire to photograph President Polk and his cabinet was finally fulfilled in the spring or early summer of 1846. By that time Polk had assumed the role of commander in chief of all U.S. military forces and was conducting a distant war. Though obviously preoccupied with matters of national consequence, the president and his advisers assembled in the State Dining Room—Thomas Jefferson's old office—to pose for Professor Plumbe. All were present except one—the secretary of state, James Buchanan.

Seated in the front row at far left is the relaxed and engaging attorney general, John Y. Mason, a Virginian who served as navy secretary for John Tyler's administration. He would play an important role in concluding the Mexican War. Next to him sat the busy secretary of war, William L. Marcy, from New York. His offhand remark "to the victors belong the spoils" forever linked his name with the patronage system. Next we see the president—somber and intense, with his hand placed across his chest, recalling a posture more familiar to the previous century. Slightly less than medium height, President Polk maintained a trim figure. His eyes were large and deep set, some said piercing as the occasion required. A shock of black hair turned gray by the time he took office was worn long and combed straight back, at times spilling over his collar. Seated at the far right is Secretary of the Treasury Robert J. Walker from Mississippi. The author of the Walker Tariff of 1846, he provided good counsel for the president and raised private funds to support the war with Mexico. The tall figure at center is Cave Johnson, a fellow Tennesseean, longtime political ally, and personal friend of the president who would serve as postmaster general throughout Polk's administration. Standing off to the side, perhaps in an unconscious effort to distance himself from the others, is Secretary of the Navy George Bancroft of Massachusetts, the preeminent American historian of his day and founder of the U.S. Naval Academy. Bancroft would bolt from Polk's cabinet in September 1846 in moral objection to the Mexican War. For his loyal service, however, Polk appointed him U.S. minister to Great Britain.

The Plumbe daguerreotype of President Polk and his cabinet holds dual historical distinctions. It is the earliest known photograph of a U.S. president with his advisers as well as the first photographic record of a room inside the White House.

Sarah Polk, according to her husband's diary, locked objecting cabinet members in the State Dining Room after lunch and made them sit for the photographer John Plumbe Jr. The result was this remarkable view of President Polk and his cabinet on the eve of the Mexican War and the first known interior photograph of the White House.

William Seale, an architectural historian, examined the interior of the White House represented in this daguerreotype and made some amazing observations. He noted that the photograph shows white-painted woodwork, which was customary throughout the house, and a highly figured, though not strongly contrasting wallpaper. The State Dining Room chairs appear in this group portrait. These were in the mode popularly known as "French antique" or Louis Quatorze. The carpeting is decorated with a flower pattern. In the background can be seen one of the marble mantels that President James Monroe ordered from Italy. Reflected in the huge mirror is the impression of a basketlike chandelier made of glass beads.[3] These are the earliest photographic records of the furnishings in the White House.

Other photographers prevailed upon President Polk for his portrait and were granted sittings. In February 1849 Mathew Brady, the future Civil War photographer, came to the White House and secured a handsome half-length portrait of the resolute president. The original daguerreotype likeness is in the Photographic Collection of the Library of Congress.

President Polk was the first chief executive to be repeatedly photographed. His willingness to accommodate photographers, even welcoming them into the White House, tells of his sense of historical awareness. Through the perseverance and artistry of pioneer photographers John Plumbe Jr., George P. A. Healy, Mathew Brady, and others, a vivid and personal record of the White House and the illustrious "dark horse" has been preserved for future generations.

LIBRARY OF CONGRESS

Mathew Brady, who would achieve great fame for his Civil War photographs, took this daguerreotype portrait of President James K. Polk near the end of his administration.

NOTES

1. James K. Polk, February 27, 1846, *Diary of James K. Polk,* ed. Milo Milton Quaife (Chicago: McClurg, 1910), 1: 391–92.

2. James K. Polk, diary, June 16, 1846, ibid., 4: 372.

3. William Seale, *The President's House* (Washington, D.C.: White House Historical Association, 1986), 254; see also Seale, editorial, *Nineteenth Century Magazine* 2 (Spring 1976): 4–5.

The White House when President Lincoln moved in on March 4, 1861, had changed very little externally since 1830, when the North Portico, shown here about 1860, was completed. From the window over the north door the president addressed nighttime "serenaders" who assembled in great numbers and "called him out" to speak.

Chapter 4

The Lincoln White House
Stage for the Republic's Survival

JEAN BAKER

THE day after Abraham Lincoln's soulful inaugural plea on March 4, 1861, that the North and South must not divide the political house that the Union represented to this generation of Americans, his wife, Mary Todd Lincoln, took measure of her new home. She was not impressed. Granted that the Executive Mansion, as it was mostly called in these days, had thirty-one rooms and was larger than any home in which the Lincolns had lived. Still, like most observers, she found the White House disappointing, full of "abominable" furniture unworthy of "the humblest cabin," peeling wallpaper, and tawdry decorations unacceptable in a simple Springfield home. "Seedy and dilapidated," reported Mary Lincoln's outspoken cousin Lizzie Grimsley.[1] In the opinion of these two sharp-eyed housewives from a prairie town, the mansion's only elegance appeared in the East, Blue, and Red Rooms, with their moldings, frescoed ceilings, and carefully drawn proportions.

But threadbare rugs, soiled upholstery, and faded curtains diminished the grandeur of these public rooms. As Grimsley reported to friends in Springfield, even "the family apartments are in a deplorably shabby condition as to furniture which looked as if it had been brought in by the first president."[2] As for the china, a preliminary investigation of the State Dining Room revealed that no more than ten guests could be served on a set of china that matched.

From 1861 to 1865, the executive business of a nation engaged in a brutal war took place mostly in a large room with a southern exposure on the second floor. Farther down the hall were the family quarters, consisting of only seven rooms, with the president's bedroom in the southwest corner, his wife's adjoining, and Tad and Willie's bedrooms across the hall. Like the ceremonial state rooms downstairs, these, too, had been neglected. By all accounts from those who visited the second

45

Illustration from Frank Leslie's Illustrated Newspaper, *March 1861, showing Abraham Lincoln's inauguration.*

floor, the family rooms were meagerly furnished with inferior furniture, relics from the days of James Monroe's administration.

Lincoln's predecessor, James Buchanan, was a bachelor, and Harriet Lane, his niece and brilliant hostess, had done little general redecorating. She had purchased some gold spoons for the elegant tea parties she gave, recalling her earlier triumphs at St. James's, and ordered the commissioner of public buildings to auction off James and Elizabeth Monroe's 1817 contribution to the Blue Room, a distinguished suite of gilded sofas, pier tables, and chairs by the Parisian cabinetmaker Pierre-Antoine Bellangé, but in 1860 they brought only $325. Harriet Lane replaced these furnishings with a very ornate set of gold-leafed, heavily carved furniture more fashionable to her own time.[3]

The ladies from Springfield were not alone in their disappointment. The

Illustration from Frank Leslie's Illustrated Newspaper, *March 1861, showing the Republican triumph at Lincoln's inaugural ball.*

place—upstairs and downstairs—reminded William Stoddard, a White House secretary, "of an old and unsuccessful hotel."[4] The walls were bare, leading the reporter
Noah Brooks to hope, unrealistically, that Congress would appropriate money for
"a few pictures by the best American artists."[5] John Nicolay, another Lincoln secretary, wondered "how long a great nation would compel its ruler to live in a small
and dilapidated shanty and in such shabby genteel style."[6]

Of course Mary and Abraham Lincoln were not strangers to the White House.
The couple had lived in Washington during his congressional term from 1847 to
1849. But during the Civil War, for all its tattiness, the White House took on an
added significance—both symbolically and in reality. In that peculiar American
arrangement that has often affected our politics as well as the personal lives of our
presidents and their families, it remained three things. First, the White House was

Abraham Lincoln's secretary John Nicolay poses in the White House greenhouse with visitors, including Plains Indians, soon after the beginning of the Civil War.

a home for the president's family, providing what architects call private space for the domestic life of the first family. In this capacity it would be the home—and occasionally school—and playground for the Lincoln sons. After Eddie's death in 1850 from tuberculosis, three Lincoln sons survived. Nineteen-year-old Robert Lincoln was at Harvard during this period, although he visited during his vacations; eleven-year-old Willie would die of typhoid fever in the Prince of Wales Bedroom across the hall from his parents' room in February 1862; and the irrepressible nine-year-old Thomas—or Taddie as he was generally known—romped through the White House and once waved a Confederate flag from the roof.

The White House also served as the workplace of the president, a fact that its name the Executive Mansion was meant to convey. It was here that the presidential business of the nation took place, and this included not only cabinet meetings and consultations with Republican officials as well as congressmen and senators but hearing the pleas of the patronage-seekers who clamored for a presidential post. During the Civil War the national government expanded rapidly, and Lincoln controlled 1,500 presidential appointments. The power of the presidency with its constitutional grant of command of the armed forces augmented a role that in peacetime was, during the nineteenth century, little more than that of an administrator. From Lincoln's office upstairs, most of the execution and planning of the war proceeded. Generals were hired and fired; strategic plans of military operations were considered; and documents including the Emancipation Proclamation and the Thirteenth Amendment were drafted.

Sometimes invisible in previous administrations was a third function—the ceremonial roles that the White House played. These consisted of state receptions and diplomatic and cabinet dinners as well as the so-called soirees that punctuated the Lincolns' life in the White House. In the past such entertainment had less political importance. But during the Civil War, as a statement of the viability of the government, White House ceremonies enabled the people to see and meet a leader whose power and influence were so enhanced during the war. By separating these functions—perhaps more sensibly for those involved—the Europeans create different buildings for such activities and different officers to fulfill them. But in the United States, the White House continues to fill several purposes, all carried on in the same place.

To her credit, Mary Lincoln immediately grasped the importance of her home to the nation. Just as the domeless United States Capitol conveyed the sense of an unfinished republic of which the war was a bloody representation, so a shabby President's House would display the powerlessness of a chief executive to foreign ministers such as Britain's Lord Lyon and France's Henri Mercier. These two diplomats as well as others stationed in Washington knew far grander architectural statements of public power in Paris's Tuileries, Madrid's Palacio Real, and London's Buckingham Palace. Because some Europeans were predisposed to recognize the Confederacy, even a symbolic weakness in the North would lead them to nudge their governments toward a prosouthern stance. Such recognition followed by military and naval aid particularly from the Queen's Navy, intent on ending Lincoln's blockade, would surely have tipped the balance to the Confederacy and arguably have led to the division of the Union into two separate nations. No other first lady has faced, and comprehended, the significance of the White House to public affairs as did Mary Lincoln during the Civil War, when the building became a stage she set for the survival of the republic.

Mary Todd Lincoln in a ball gown, photographed by Mathew Brady, ca. 1862.

Newspaper illustration of the White House garden party, July 21, 1861, for Prince Napoleon (Joseph Charles Paul Bonaparte), a nephew of the Emperor Napoleon III, who was in America ostensibly to view military maneuvers in the Civil War for his imperial uncle. He was, in fact, escaping a duel. For all the joy in the picture, the Union suffered a defeat that same day at Bull Run. From Frank Leslie's Illustrated Newspaper, *July 1861, tinted by P. Hall Baglie.*

With characteristic energy Mary Lincoln turned immediately to the job of transforming the dismal interior of the President's home into a demonstration that improved all three aspects of this building's functions—domestic, executive, and ceremonial. After Lincoln's inauguration she was initially delayed by the threat of a Confederate attack on Washington that resulted in the stationing at the White House of a company of Frontier Guards and Zouaves (the latter a troop of New Yorkers under Colonel Elmer Ellsworth who took their name from and dressed in the exotic outfits of Algerian soldiers). And even as other wives of officials were leaving vulnerable Washington for their safer homes, she went to New York in the dangerous spring of 1861 to search for the best wallpaper, rugs, china, and crystal. Traveling with the commissioner of public buildings and her friend and cousin

Lizzie Grimsley, she led the way into the best stores in New York and Philadelphia. From Philadelphia she dispatched a merchant to buy wallpaper in Paris, and from Alexander Stewart's new department store in New York she ordered in a record day's shopping $2,000 worth of rugs and curtains. Twice more in 1861 Mary Lincoln undertook buying expeditions to New York, and during her tenure as first lady she made as many as ten such trips.

It took some time for the completion of her task, especially in the East Room, where the Zouaves had regularly presented arms, denting the floor and sometimes even discharging their muskets, to Tad's delight, into the walls. In the Blue Room the arrival of the French wallpaper was delayed. Eventually the results were spectacular, but because interior decoration is ephemeral and temporary, Mary Lincoln's tasteful redecoration has been overlooked in the assessment of the Lincolns' contributions to the White House.

Mary Lincoln did not choose to buy much furniture, although this would be the hallmark of future internal improvements superintended by first ladies. Instead, some furniture was repaired, and other pieces, discovered in the attic and closets of the White House, were revarnished. She did buy for the upstairs Prince of Wales Bedroom an ornate mahogany bed with rosewood carvings—soon to become very famous—and a Victorian canopy of queenly proportions. She also purchased a 190-piece set of fine Limoges porcelain decorated with royal purple and double lines of gilt, with the seal of the United States on each piece. With politics never far away from either Abraham's or Mary Lincoln's mind, the gold border was entwined with two lines signifying the union of North and South.

Soon even past critics of the White House who, like the Ohio senator's wife Mrs. Donn Piatt, had earlier found the mansion "miserable," were complimenting the first lady on her redecoration.[7] Europeans, usually so snooty about any pretensions in this backwater republic of the people, were also impressed. Ernest Duvergier de Hauranne, a French traveler who visited the Lincoln White House, was pleased by the mansion but astonished that no one needed a formal invitation or a frock coat to be admitted: "The servants don't have the authority to refuse admittance on the grounds even of muddy boots or disreputable clothes to any patriotic citizen eager to meet his president."[8] A New York soldier stationed in Washington wrote home with surprise that "every person has a right to go through the rooms of the White House."[9]

But the costs of this refurbishing ran high in terms of Mary Lincoln's reputation as well as the budget. In the past the commissioner of public buildings had supervised any refurbishing and redecorating on a budget of $20,000 for four years,

Colonel Elmer Ellsworth's funeral in the East Room, May 1861. Ellsworth volunteered to guard
President-elect Abraham Lincoln, and the family quickly took him in as one of their own. He lived in the
family quarters at the White House. When he was shot dead during the taking of Alexandria across the
river by Union troops, the Lincolns held his funeral "at home" at the White House. Ellsworth was the first
Union casualty of note in the Civil War. This sketch is probably by the news artist Alfred R. Waud.

along with an annual $6,000 for repairs. Usually he did this alone, with little coun-
sel or advice from the first lady. But Mary Lincoln lived when increasing numbers
of consumer goods were assembled for sale in vast emporiums like Alexander
Stewart's marble department store in New York. By 1860 many middle-class American women were taking greater authority over domestic matters because their
husbands worked away from home. The housewife was the one now doing the
buying and shopping. Defined as "domestic feminism," the control of women over
their homes became fairly typical in cities. This was even more true in households
inhabited by men like Abraham Lincoln who were uninterested in such details as
interior decoration. Thus Mary Lincoln became a prime practitioner of what was
going on elsewhere throughout the United States, although her home was a special one—"the People's House," as the press sometimes called it.

By 1862 Mary Lincoln had overspent the congressional allotment, and with no
understanding of the possibilities of enlisting the help of private donors (save for

her dresses), she was overbudget at a time when most national resources necessarily went for the war. Her husband was angry as well. Pronouncing the White House the best house in which they had ever lived, the president complained that her shopping would "stink" throughout the land and that she must take personal responsibility for her "flub-a-dubs."[10]

Yet, in many ways, the benefit to the nation was worth the cost, as the public ceremonial rooms of the White House emerged as effective statements of the power of the Union government as well as of the authority of its chief executive, whose election had led to the secession of the South. The Lincolns used all the great rooms of the first floor of the White House for entertaining not just Washington society, Congress, the courts, and the diplomatic corps; they also entertained a cross section of the American people, and especially the nation's soldiers, who flocked to their receptions to meet the president and his wife. Often the lines for receptions stretched out the door; the coatrooms were full, and the Lincolns suffered bruises and aches after three and four hours of shaking hands with an eager citizenry. Given the endless parades of people, receptions designated to last until 11:00 P.M. sometimes continued until after midnight. "Fortunately," commented Hauranne, "Lincoln was a farmer and his hands can take the terrible punishment."[11]

Left unsupervised during their visits, the people pulled samples of the new wallpaper from the walls, scissored the heavy cord and tassels from the new crimson hangings in the East Room, and managed on one occasion to steal an entire lace curtain.[12] Visitors to the White House cut small bits of Mary Lincoln's new carpet, leaving scars on the floor below. By 1863 the reception crowds grew so great that it was necessary to call the metropolitan police to prevent vandalism and the taking of mementos. Eventually, to restrain the ambitious crew of Washington pickpockets, all coats and wraps had to be left in the front vestibule.

Despite the damage, these parties were significant at a time when the morale of the people could be enhanced by a meeting with the president. Instinctively the Lincolns seemed to recognize this, and during the sixteenth president's administration the doors of the White House opened as the People's House. Ralph Waldo Emerson noted that "at last a middle-class country has a middle-class president."[13]

Of the receptions, one of the longtime doormen of the White House, William Crook, wrote, "President and Mrs. Lincoln stood in the octagonal [sic] Blue Room near the West door. Guests entered from the left through the Red Room. The Lincolns received in the Blue Room and the guests went through the Green Room to the Great East Room. . . . It was all bright and gay." This same guard who served nine presidents from Lincoln to Theodore Roosevelt believed that the White House was "never so entirely given over to the public as during Mr. Lincoln's Administration. The times were too tense to make of social affairs anything other than an aid to more serious matters."[14] And so the Lincolns used the great public rooms of the downstairs to meet the American people, more than two thousand of whom fought to get into what became the couple's last public reception, on March 4, 1865, after Lincoln's second inauguration. Overall, Americans were impressed with this accessible president's unaffected nature, his simple manners, and his dignity, which many noted was tinged with kindness. They were also impressed with the style and grace of his wife on what the Lincolns referred to privately as their "Handshake Days."

In the dining room on the west end of the building, the Lincolns used their new china during official dinners when, sitting across from each other in the middle of the table, they entertained leaders of Congress and the diplomatic corps at state dinners. Fresh flowers were considered one of Mary Lincoln's novel contributions. There was no dancing—it was considered inappropriate during wartime—but the Marine Band often played, sometimes including a special new piece, "The Mary Lincoln Polka." William Henry Russell, the correspondent for the *London Times,* dismissed these affairs as without splendor and without liveried servants and with dishes that may be called "Gallo-American, and wines that owed their parentage to France and their rearing and education in the United States."[15] Others, usually Americans, were nonetheless impressed with the conviviality of the first lady and the care with which she entertained, as well as her endurance.

While these allegiance-gathering, patriotism-suffusing celebrations took place in the downstairs rooms, the endless toil of the chief executive went on upstairs in the middle room of the three-room office suite, facing southward. Here Lincoln worked in an office that measured twenty-five by thirty feet, with a marble fireplace in the center on the west side, a bust of the Democrat Andrew Jackson that never bothered the Republican Lincoln, an oak table in the center, and the large windows from which one could see Arlington Heights and the Confederacy. The only new furniture in the room was a rack that held the war maps on which Lincoln depended as he became a quick study on military matters. In his office the chairs were rickety, the horsehair sofa uncomfortable, the accessories nonexistent, and the atmosphere Spartan. One of the ironies of the Lincoln White House was that in this vast building which was the Executive Mansion more space was not de-

Mathew Brady photographed Abraham Lincoln and his son Tad thumbing through an album.

voted to the president's official business. Instead, the ceremonial and family rooms predominated in size and number, perhaps reflecting the state of a presidency whose principal functions before the war had been to dispense patronage, attend intermittently to foreign policy, and sign bills developed and passed by Congress.

The seven members of Lincoln's cabinet who seemed to have immediate access to the president any time met formally on Tuesdays and Fridays, with at least one member—Salmon P. Chase—perhaps lost in reverie about how he might conspire to replace Lincoln at the next election. Here discussions on military and

Abraham Lincoln sits with his two secretaries, John Nicolay, left, and John Hay. Photograph by Mathew Brady.

financial policy proceeded, often with many interruptions because of Lincoln's de-
terminedly open presidency. Here with only the Bible, copies of the United States
Statutes and the Constitution, and the plays of Shakespeare as reference books, this
wartime president made his decisions, wrote his state messages, and directed the
vast operation of the Civil War.

But the disposition and placing of these rooms interfered with the nation's
business, for Lincoln's two energetic secretaries, John Nicolay and John Hay, slept
and worked in rooms on the second floor on the east and could not intercept the
callers and patronage-seekers who came up the office staircase. Remembering that
he had once been a patronage-seeker himself, the president graciously met those
who begged for favors in the reception room next to his office, in what Lincoln
called "the Beggar's Opera." Lincoln had little privacy and often took refuge in his
secretaries' bedroom.

Surely the biggest nuisance for the hardworking president involved the patronage-seekers who continued to beg for the government jobs that Lincoln could
bestow. Only in 1863 did the doorkeeper begin to sequester them in a downstairs
office, and even then hundreds of favor-seekers broke loose unless under guard,
scrambling up the stairs to Lincoln's office, camping out in the thickly crowded
hall, and requiring Mary Lincoln and the children to step over them if they wanted
to walk to their rooms. In fact, the only structural change that the Lincolns made
to the White House was to create a temporary passage from his office through the
reception room into the oval family library, so that the president would not have
to pass through the outer corridor full of supplicants.

One of the criticisms of this administration was the time that Lincoln accorded
to "the endless requests of poor widows who wanted to work in the Treasury Department, the brigadiers who wanted a promotion, the inventors after a contract,
and the curiosity seekers with an autograph book."[16] When a delegation of veterans
from the War of 1812 visited him in 1862, the president confessed that he had not a
minute to prepare a "pretty speech, or any sort of speech" and complained of "the
continual and intense engrossment" of his time "by very trying circumstances."[17]
One example of the outrageous demands on his time was his meeting with a temperance society during which he encountered three "blue-skinned damsels representing Love, Purity and Fidelity" and listened to a long speech from their leaders
who believed that drink was impeding the Union Army's success. All of this, to Lincoln's amusement, was observed by his half-tipsy coachman.[18]

The president also spent many working hours outside the White House in the
adjacent War Department, where there was a telegraph office and he could hear

PLATE 1. John Adams, *by John Trumbull, ca. 1793. Painted while Adams was vice president, this flattering portrait evokes in an almost ethereal way the intelligence of the statesman who would, in 1800, be the first president to occupy the White House.*

PLATE 2.
Abigail Smith Adams
(Mrs. John Adams),
completed by Gilbert Stuart,
1815. Abigail Adams found
the new President's House
an unfinished "castle."

PLATE 3.
Sèvres porcelain, part of a
dinner set purchased by John
and Abigail Adams while he
was the American minister
to France and used for official
entertaining during his
presidency.

PLATE 4. Dolley Madison, *by Gilbert Stuart, 1804. Dolley Madison brought her White House years to a melo-dramatic climax in her flight from the invading British in a carriage packed with official papers, believed to include the Constitution and Declaration of Independence. The consummate hostess, she demonstrated for generations to come the great public appeal of a first lady's personal touch in White House living.*

PLATE 5. President James Madison, *by John Vanderlyn, 1816. The genius behind the Constitution, James Madison was a shrewd politician who made use of the White House to court members of Congress on both sides of the aisle.*

PLATE 6. *Furnishings for the "Elliptical Saloon," by Benjamin Henry Latrobe, 1809. The Madisons in 1809 commissioned the architect Benjamin Henry Latrobe to redecorate a suite of White House rooms for entertaining, including the oval one we today call the Blue Room. Such very British decorative ideas as these "Grecian" sofas and chairs received great acclaim even in the shadow of war with England. The furniture and central heating system installed with the suite were lost when the house was burned during the siege of Washington in 1814.*

PLATE 7.

George Washington, *by Gilbert Stuart, 1797. The oldest artifact of continuous use in the White House, this painting was displayed first in the dining room, then in the Red Room, and, beginning in 1929, in the East Room, where it hangs today. George Washington sat for Gilbert Stuart in Philadelphia during his presidency for the original of this portrait, commissioned by a British peer. He wears the black velvet suit he wore at his formal levees. On the table is the artificial hat—a front only—that he carried at the levees to avoid shaking hands, a custom he thought inappropriate to the head of state.*

PLATE 8.
*Ruins of the White
House, watercolor by
George Munger, 1814.
Only the stone walls
remained and many
of those were
partially replaced.*

PLATE 9. The President's House, Washington, *watercolor by Lefevre J. Cranstone, ca. 1860. Lincoln's White House is seen from the south, where the wall-enclosed grounds were open to the public from time to time but only at the president's pleasure. These were as close to a private park as the president had. Major B. B. French, the commissioner of public buildings, rigged up the terra-cotta fountain, which never operated properly. The sweeping "Jefferson Mounds," much exaggerated here, were composed of earth from the cellars of the Treasury extension next door.*

PLATE 10.

First Reading of the Emancipation
Proclamation, *by Francis Bicknell
Carpenter, 1864. The artist spent six months
in the White House, and, with Abraham
Lincoln's full cooperation, he was able to
achieve accuracy in every detail of this
painting.*

PLATE 11.

U.S. Grant and His Family, *by William
Cogswell, 1867. This picture, certainly one
with a purpose, shared the Red Room walls
with Gilbert Stuart's* Washington *and
defined the Grants as an ideal American
family. It was brought to the White House in
a wagon from the Grants' home soon after the
inauguration. Engravings of the family group
adorned many an American parlor through
the late nineteenth century.*

immediate reports from the battlefield. It may stretch credulity—though it is in fact the case—that there was no telegraph line into the White House during the Civil War. But then, a line had never seemed needed before. Without this electronic link to the battlefield, Lincoln worked mostly in his upstairs office and reception room. Sprung from the prairies, he needed little grandeur or comfort to concentrate on the war, which he did without vacation and with very little leisure, save for some time spent at Anderson Cottage, on the grounds of the Soldiers' Home—his summer and fall White House.

The third function that the White House served was as a home to the Lincoln family, and in this regard the private quarters on the west end of the second floor—the Lincolns' adjoining bedrooms on the south side and the boys' bedrooms across the hall on the north side—were private space. So, too, was the White House sitting room or library situated directly above the Blue Room. The first lady's bedroom served as an office where Mary Lincoln kept up with her correspondence, worried about the bills for her expensive clothes, and played with the boys. She, too, was busier than she had ever been. "If you were aware how much every moment is occupied, you would excuse me" became a standard excuse to friends whose letters went unanswered for months.[19]

While her husband was home more than he ever had been in the past, the president was also not at home at all, given his prodigious hours of attending to the proliferating business of the nation. Mary Lincoln once wrote, "I feel myself lucky if by eleven o'clock he is ready to join me in my chamber."[20] Accustomed to life in the nosy, gossipy capital town of Springfield, this Illinois couple was more isolated than it had ever been before; at the same time, the Lincolns were on very public display. Still, among their diversions was playing with the boys, and several observers arrived in the White House to find the president on the floor serving as a horse, his sons astride his thin frame, kicking his sides and calling, "Geddy-Up, Geddy-Up."

Tad and Willie enjoyed, as their mother and father did not, every part of the drafty White House—its public ceremonial downstairs rooms, its upstairs private quarters, its attic full of broken relics from other administrations, as well as their father's office. The Lincolns were the first White House family since the Tylers to raise young children in the Executive Mansion. Changes in the understanding of child raising and family life encouraged interest in the antics of the boys, who amused an American public reveling in the private life of its chief executive—Tad aiming a toy cannon at the cabinet, Tad finding and disrupting the White House bell system, Tad and Willie dressing up their beloved goat Nanko and hitching her

Anderson Cottage at the Soldiers' Home, 1863. The Soldiers' Home was an estate purchased for the purpose its name suggests by General Winfield Scott with prize money he received for the capture of Mexico City. James Buchanan conscripted the main residence as a summer place, as did Abraham Lincoln and other presidents to follow.

to a wagon that they proudly led through a reception in the East Room, Tad and Willie eating the strawberries intended for a state dinner. But as they never had been in their younger years in Springfield, these boys were isolated from their contemporaries, despite their mother's effort to encourage visits from especially the Taft brothers, who lived nearby.

Ultimately, the personal grief suffered by other Americans descended on the private Lincoln White House in the loss of a son. In February 1862 Willie Lincoln, most beloved of his parents, died of typhoid fever after a long illness. Some said he died from bilious fever or a malarial infection. Most believed the third Lincoln son died from fecally contaminated water. Since the 1830s the president's household had its drinking water piped in from a spring-fed pond; other water used in the White House came directly from the Potomac River, where night soil was often dumped. During the war, when Washington's normal population swelled to 200,000 and the army set up camps without latrine trenches, the Potomac became a vast septic tank. Its lethal contents were piped into White House lavatories, from which a child might innocently drink.

As it has for all first families, the White House altered the life of the family who lived there from 1861 to 1865. When they arrived, the Lincolns understood that the White House was not a permanent home, although after Lincoln's victory in 1864 they expected to stay for another four years. As the president explained to an Ohio regiment in 1864, he was only the current resident of the Executive Mansion and the peaceful rotation of the office was what the war was about. "I happen temporarily to occupy this big White House. I am a living witness that any one of your children may look to come here as my father's child has. . . . It is for this the struggle should be maintained, that we may not lose our birthright."[21]

Every member of the Lincoln family had for one reason or another enjoyed the grandeur of the building and its public significance. But privately, life in the White House devastated the little band of five who had taken up residence in March 1861. Mary Lincoln, Robert, and Tad would remember forever that Willie's body had lain in its metal coffin in the Green Room, and three years later, Lincoln's own funeral took place in the East Room. Robert attended this final event, but Mary Lincoln, Tad at her side, remained upstairs, too grief-stricken to be in the same room where she and her husband had in better days enjoyed the grand receptions that had kept the family in touch with ordinary Americans. In the Civil War White House, the private life of a family and the public duties of a president and first lady sadly and irrevocably merged. Just as war had taken 600,000 lives from the nation, the White House claimed its casualties from the Lincoln family.

Robert Todd Lincoln, at about the time he joined the army. Photograph by Mathew Brady, ca. 1864.

NOTES

1. Mary Todd Lincoln to Alex Williamson, January 26, 1866, in *Mary Todd Lincoln: Her Life and Letters,* ed. Justin G. Turner and Linda Levitt Turner (New York: Alfred A. Knopf, 1972), 330; "Elizabeth Grimsley, Six Months in the White House," *Journal of the Illinois State Historical Society* 19 (October 1926–January 1927), 47.

2. "Grimsley," 47.

3. William G. Allman, "Furnishing the Executive Mansion: Nineteenth-Century Washington Sources," in *Our Changing White House,* ed. Wendell Garrett (Boston: Northeastern University Press, 1995), 149.

4. William O. Stoddard, *Inside the White House in War Times: Memoirs and Reports of Lincoln's Secretary,* ed. Michael Burlingame (Lincoln: University of Nebraska Press, 2000), 49.

5. Quoted in http//www.mrlincolnswhitehouse.org/content/html.

6. Quoted in Harry Pratt and Ernest East, "Mrs. Lincoln Refurbishes the White House," *Lincoln Lore* 47 (February 1945): 12–22.

7. Turner and Turner, *Mary Todd Lincoln,* 106.

8. Ralph Bowen, ed., *Ernest Duvergier de Hauranne: A Frenchman in Lincoln's America* (Chicago: Donnelly, 1975), 357.

9. Quoted in William Davis, *Lincoln's Men* (New York: Free Press, 1993), 59.

10. Jean H. Baker, *Mary Todd Lincoln: A Biography* (New York: W. W. Norton, 1987), 188–89.

11. Bowen, *Hauranne,* 345.

12. Margaret Leech, *Reveille in Washington* (New York: Harpers & Brothers, 1941), 357.

13. Quoted in Burton Bledstein, *The Culture of Professionalism: The Middle Class and the Development of Higher Education* (New York: W. W. Norton, 1976), 30.

14. Colonel William Crook, *Through Five Administrations: Reminiscences of Colonel William H. Crook,* ed. Margarita Gerry (New York: Harper & Brothers, 1910), 17. Crook, in fact, served nine presidents.

15. William Howard Russell, *My Diary, North and South* (New York: Harper, 1954), 29.

16. Noah Brooks, *Washington in Lincoln's Time* (New York: Century, 1895), 248–49.

17. Quoted in Mark Neely, *The Last Best Hope of Earth: Abraham Lincoln and the Promise of America* (Cambridge, Mass.: Harvard University Press, 1993), 109.

18. Roy Basler, ed., *Collected Works of Abraham Lincoln* (New Brunswick, N.J.: Rutgers University Press, 1953), 7:487–88.

19. Turner and Turner, *Mary Todd Lincoln,* 81, 202, 206.

20. Ibid., 187.

21. Basler, *Collected Works of Abraham Lincoln,* 7:512.

A sentry on duty during the Civil War. The north grounds of the White House were partitioned by iron fencing that in theory controlled public access from the street and within the grounds. Visitors were allowed to view the house and the small garden plot in front of it at certain times, but to move any closer involved passing guard stations.

Chapter 5

Images of the Executive Mansion, 1861–1865

BETTY C. MONKMAN

T HE crisis of the Civil War focused the attention of the American people on President Abraham Lincoln, Washington, D.C., and the White House. As part of the increased news coverage, artists and photographers sought to capture and publish visual images of the president, his family and staff, the White House, and the dramatic events taking place at the center of the presidency. Twenty-two years after the introduction of the earliest type of photograph, the daguerreotype, photographers were limited to documenting the exterior of the house and its grounds, as early photographic technology all but precluded recording interior spaces outside the confines of the photographic portrait studio. Lincoln sat for several photo sessions in the Washington studios of Mathew Brady and Alexander Gardner, but it was left to artists and illustrators to execute drawings and paintings of White House events and rooms. Some of these were published in popular illustrated newspapers such as *Harper's Weekly* and *Frank Leslie's Illustrated Newspaper,* where the war and the momentous events of Lincoln's presidency were recorded for an American public hungry for news. The White House and its surrounding grounds were depicted in 1860 by a visiting English artist, Lefevre J. Cranstone, in a watercolor from the south; the scene is as it appeared when the Lincoln family took up residence. The American landscape painter Albert Bierstadt painted a view looking south from the President's House toward the Potomac about 1863.

PLATE 9

In the early months of the war, volunteers arrived in Washington to protect the Executive Mansion, as the White House was then officially called, and the Capitol. They were photographed and sketched as they drilled on the South Lawn, paraded before the North Portico on Pennsylvania Avenue, and encamped in the East Room. In the summer of 1861, the English illustrator Alfred R. Waud drew, in pencil and ink, Lincoln's first review of troops arriving from the north. Throughout

Only one photograph depicts a state room from the Lincoln era. This stereographic view of the East Room, with its chandeliers from Andrew Jackson's administration and frescoed ceiling decoration from Franklin Pierce, is seen as it appeared after Mary Todd Lincoln added new carpet and wallpaper.

the war, artists chronicled military reviews and notable events hosted by Abraham and Mary Todd Lincoln in the state rooms and on the grounds. Only one other visual source exists for Lincoln's East Room, a stereographic view taken about 1865–66, showing it extensively refurbished by Mary Todd Lincoln in 1861.

Shortly after the attack on Fort Sumter in April 1861, the first volunteers arrived to protect the White House and the Capitol. President Lincoln was photographed on the South Lawn with the Clay Battalion, organized by the Kentucky abolitionist Cassius M. Clay.

From beneath an awning placed on the sidewalk on the north side of the White House, President Abraham Lincoln and General Winfield Scott review a parade of three-year volunteers. Drawing by Alfred R. Waud, 1861.

68

Early in 1864 the painter Francis Bicknell Carpenter requested permission to paint President Lincoln in his office for the artist's depiction of the first reading of the Emancipation Proclamation before the Cabinet. Lincoln not only sat for sketches but showed Carpenter the seated positions occupied by the Cabinet at the reading. Carpenter also arranged for Anthony Berger of Mathew Brady's studio to photograph Lincoln in his office, the only photographs taken of Lincoln in the White House. Two photographs of this sitting survive: one of Lincoln seated at the south end of the table, and the other of him standing near the end of the table.

The sparsely landscaped north front of the Executive Maansion, ca. 1860–1865, provided a full view of the 1857 greenhouse on the right (also see page 48). For Lincoln and his successors for forty years the "glass house" was a peaceful retreat from the crowded White House.

Lincoln's second floor office, also used for cabinet meetings, was one of the most thoroughly documented offices of a nineteenth-century president until the late 1880s, when interior photography had been refined with new technology. Lincoln generously allowed artists access to his work space, and in the winter of 1864 he granted the artist Francis B. Carpenter unlimited time to record the details of his office for his painting of the first reading of the Emancipation Proclamation before

The most detailed depiction of President Lincoln's office was drawn by the illustrator Charles K. Stellwagen in the fall of 1864. Lincoln's desk was located between the windows with his chair, covered in black haircloth, in front of the window to the right. A portrait of Andrew Jackson by Miner K. Kellogg that had been in the White House for more than two decades hung over the mantel. Beneath it stood a French black marble mantel clock purchased for the White House by Jackson.

the cabinet. In preparation, Carpenter arranged for the only photographs taken of Lincoln in the White House. He engaged Anthony Berger, who worked for Brady, to record Lincoln seated at the cabinet table in front of the mantel, the pose Carpenter used in composing his painting. A second photograph of Lincoln portrays him standing at the end of the table and reveals additional details of a different part of the office. These blurred images of Lincoln, along with several of Carpenter's

President and Mrs. Lincoln received their guests in the oval Blue Room on New Year's Day, 1863, when President Lincoln shook thousands of hands. Shortly after the end of this annual open house, he retired to his office, where, with swollen hand, he steadily put his signature to the seminal document of his administration, the Emancipation Proclamation.

sketches of particulars such as carpet and drapery designs, constitute a visual record of sections of the office. (Carpenter's sketches remain with his descendants.) In the fall of 1864 the illustrator Charles K. Stellwagen rendered a fuller perspective of the room that shows one wall covered with maps of Virginia, Charleston harbor, and Kentucky and the placement of desks and other furnishings.

These photographs, prints, and paintings, supplemented by reporters' descriptions of the President's House and the activities of the presidency, conveyed visual images of the Lincoln White House to a nation gripped by the cataclysmic Civil War.

PLATE 10

A rare view of the Red Room as completed by President Chester A. Arthur in 1882. Notice Julia Dent Grant's Herter Brothers armchair, right (see page 88). Photograph by Frances Benjamin Johnston, 1889.

The Gold
in the Gilded Age

RICHARD NORTON SMITH

THE years from Appomattox to San Juan Hill—roughly bracketed by the soldier-turned-politician Ulysses S. Grant and the politician–turned–soldier Theodore Roosevelt—have become synonymous in popular and scholarly imagination alike with parvenu wealth, stifling convention, and officially sanctioned thievery. In a mock catechism written two years before his minor novel, *The Gilded Age,* inadvertently christened the era, Mark Twain scolded his materialistic countrymen. "What is the chief end of man?" asked Twain in September 1871. "To get rich. In what way? Dishonestly if we can; honestly if we must. Who is God, the one and only and true? Money is God. Gold and greenbacks and stock—father, son and the ghost of same."[1]

Chief executives might come and go, but whatever inhabitant temporarily called the White House home could rely on the sardonic disapproval of Henry Adams, his neighbor across Lafayette Square. According to Adams, one could conclusively disprove Darwinian theories of evolution simply by tracing the line of presidents from Washington to Grant. It is a bon mot long since enshrined by Adams's academic and literary descendants.

Writing in the 1930s, Thomas Wolfe dismissed the parade of former Civil War generals who went on to occupy the White House as the lost Americans "whose gravely vacant bewhiskered faces mixed, melted, swam together. . . . Which had the whiskers," asked Wolfe, "which the burnsides: which was which?" They may have worn blue on the battlefield, Wolfe implied, but in the history books they appear relentlessly gray.[2]

There is nothing terribly surprising about this: scholars have always paid disproportionate attention to the articulate few who prefer writing books to amassing fortunes. Accordingly, while nineteenth-century reformers lost many a legislative or electoral battle, they have all but swept the field of historical assessment. Nor has the White House itself escaped guilt by association with what has been characterized as "an age of jobbery, profiteering, and false glitter." Period photographs evoke an overstuffed setting cluttered with Frances Cleveland's sofas and Chester Arthur's Tiffany glass screen. A pervasive scent of hothouse lilies and antimacassar oil supply the cloying backdrop for "bewhiskered and obscene" politicians "drooling tobacco juice" while forging an unholy alliance with amoral lobbyists and businessmen. Together this predatory coalition reduced the federal government to a nullity, which on occasion bestirred itself to reward the buccaneer, crush the wage earner, exterminate the Indian, or thwart progress toward racial equality.

So runs the conventional portrayal. Condescension, needless to say, is not the same as historical analysis. Besides its extravagance and often rigid class structure, the White House reflected postwar America's dynamism, inventiveness, and cultural flowering. There was no shortage of gold in the Gilded Age, even if some of it was fool's gold. Try to imagine, if you can, another America, a simpler, slower land whose citizens do not automatically look to Washington to solve their problems, or to the man in the White House to feel their pain. Indeed, much of their pain can be traced to greedy or shortsighted politicians who had plundered the public treasury as they squandered the moral high ground won at such terrible cost on a thousand fields of battle north and south.

Consider the fate of the last three presidents: one assassinated, another impeached, a third tainted by the corruption of his associates. Is it any wonder, then, that America in 1876 should be a land emotionally drained by a quarter-century of moral agitation, fraternal warfare, and dashed illusions? The hunger for reconciliation—even restoration—over genuine reconstruction was captured perfectly in Ulysses Grant's delphic utterance: "Let Us Have Peace." Notwithstanding a recent surge in biographical interest, Grant remains the great American puzzle. The relentless strategist who earned renown as the first exponent of modern warfare, denounced by critics then and since as a butcher, grew sick at the sight of a Mexican bullfight or an underdone steak. His horror of bloodshed was matched only by his hatred of profanity. Hopeless in civilian life, on the battlefield Grant forgot his insecurities. "Find out where your enemy is," he once explained. "Get at him as soon as you can. Strike at him as hard as you can, and keep moving on."[3]

At Shiloh and Vicksburg, Grant had no difficulty finding his enemy or striking with maximum force. In the presidency, he seemed out of his depth, a sphinxlike figure whose silences masked not hidden reserves but stubbornly misplaced loyalties. As Edmund Wilson wrote of the feverish postwar years, "It was the age of the audacious confidence man, and Grant was the incurable sucker."[4] Perhaps it is no accident that Grant's favorite book was Twain's *Innocents Abroad*. In time his name would enter the language in ways hardly imaginable to the Hero of Appomattox, as "Grantism" became a byword for official corruption. His secretary of war escaped conviction for bribery by a timely resignation. His minister to Great Britain, after marketing worthless mining stock to gullible Britons, resorted to diplomatic immunity in order to evade British justice. Grant's vice president, not to mention the Speaker of the House and a dozen other members of Congress, were implicated in the Crédit Mobilier scandal in which railroad promoters enriched themselves through millions of dollars in government bonds.

PLATE 11

Unsurprisingly, if not altogether justifiably, such peculations have left the Grant presidency in bad odor. It will come as no surprise that Julia Grant held a very different view of the "bright and beautiful dream" with which she equated her eight years in the White House. "I love the dear old house," she declared in her memoirs. Not everyone in the dear old house reciprocated. As accustomed as her soldier-husband to giving orders, on discovering the first-floor reception room crowded with messengers, sweepers, and ushers eating lunch and smoking their pipes, Julia put a stop to such practices. Henceforth employees must appear in dress suits and white gloves. Annoyed that the grounds behind the mansion were open to the public, affording her children no place to ride their velocipedes, the first lady closed the gates. On the other hand, she gave instructions to admit to her receptions any black citizens of Washington who might call. None did.[5]

In some ways the Grant White House fit the stereotype of Victorian America. Bluestockings rose up in anger when the president's teenage daughter Nellie was discovered dancing the polka in the predawn hours. Nellie Grant's 1874 wedding to a caddish young Englishman with the irresistible name of Algernon Sartoris attracted more favorable attention. So did Julia's twenty-nine-course state dinners, catered by the celebrated Washington firm of Jacob Demonet. Less successful was a White House redecoration scheme dubbed "Steamboat Gothic." If the public rooms appeared incoherent, they were as nothing compared to the private quarters. So many of Julia's in-laws resided there that one unfriendly publication declared "the Dent family ring" to be the nation's most notorious criminal mob.[6]

A Democratic father-in-law was the least of Grant's problems. Striking uncomfortably close to home was the gold-buying scandal that began with Abel Corbin, a sixty-one-year-old lobbyist who married the president's spinster sister, Virginia, for reasons having less to do with romance than with roguery. As it happened, Corbin was the agent of unscrupulous Wall Street speculators led by Jay

The reception room near the president's office, upstairs at the White House, where the Cabinet met and crowds collected to see the president for countless reasons. This watercolor by Charles Boughton was published in Frank Leslie's Illustrated Newspaper, *February 1893.*

Gould and Jim Fisk. It was said of Fisk that he was "first in war, first in peace, and first in the pockets of his countrymen." In 1869 this unholy trinity set out to corner the gold market. Having secured the appointment of a co-conspirator as head of the New York Treasury Office, and with Grant away from Washington that September, they went on a gold-buying spree, confident that no warning to the government would be issued from New York.

Their confidence, like the ensuing panic, was short-lived. Rejecting Corbin's appeal for nonintervention, Grant directed the secretary of the treasury to sell $4 million in government gold reserves. For good measure he had Julia write Corbin, warning of ruin should her brother-in-law be implicated in the scam. To this day the question of Julia's own possible involvement—raised by the timely delivery of $25,000 in cash to the first lady at the White House—remains a favorite historical parlor game. In any event, a thread of gold runs throughout the tapestry of her husband's presidency. Grant insisted that the American economy itself be gold based. Under his leadership the national debt was significantly reduced, and the United States went from a debtor to a creditor nation. The first president to call for a line-item veto, Grant issued more vetoes than all his predecessors combined, none more courageous (or politically foolhardy) than an 1874 bill to inflate the currency and thereby relieve distressed farmers.[7]

There is, however, a very different kind of gold to be mined in the Gilded Age. On Sunday, March 4, 1877, Julia Grant welcomed two thousand guests at her final White House reception. Later that Sunday night, her husband looked on as Rutherford B. Hayes was sworn into office privately in the Red Room as the nation's nineteenth president. The public inauguration would take place the following day. It would be hard to imagine less favorable circumstances for a new president than the sullen, bitterly divided nation that grudgingly acquiesced in Hayes's assumption of office. Many Democrats boycotted the ceremony, protesting the methods used to secure Hayes's victory, by a single hotly disputed electoral vote, over New York Governor Samuel J. Tilden. Critics openly mocked the man they called "His Fraudulency." Not since 1825, when John Quincy Adams was elected by the House of Representatives following allegations of a "corrupt bargain" involving the sale of the State Department, had presidential legitimacy been so in doubt. And Adams's single term had been a train wreck of embarrassments.

To Henry Adams the new president was "a third rate nonentity, whose only recommendation is that he is obnoxious to no one."[8] But appearances were deceiving. In his letter formally accepting the Republican nomination, Ohio's three-term governor had called for an overhaul of the nation's notoriously corrupt civil service. As he put it, "The reform should be thorough, radical, and complete."[9] Even more stunning was Hayes's pledge to serve but a single four-year term. Just as a century later it would take the veteran anticommunist Richard Nixon to open China, so it fell to Hayes, the amiable career politician from the Republican heartland, to plead the cause of political reform.

About this time Henry Adams recounted his unsuccessful plea with a cabinet officer to use patience and tact when dealing with members of the House of Representatives. "You can't use tact with a Congressman!" said the presidential counselor. "A Congressman is a hog! You must take a stick and hit him on the snout!" But if a congressman is a hog, thought Adams, then what is a senator? He quickly answered his own question. "The most troublesome task of a reform President was that of bringing the Senate back to decency," he concluded.[10]

Which is precisely what Rutherford Hayes set out to do in the spring of 1877.

President and Mrs. Rutherford B. Hayes by Currier & Ives, 1878.

His Inaugural Address contained the memorable declaration "He serves his party best who serves his country best." Within weeks of taking office, the new president launched an investigation into the nation's largest customhouses, where corruption and influence peddling were an expensive way of life. When a presidential commission recommended substantial reductions in staffing and an end to partisan oversight, Hayes concurred enthusiastically. Protesting Republican lawmakers staged a tense White House confrontation. From his desk drawer Hayes took a copy of the 1876 GOP platform. He invited his callers to read its pledges regarding civil service reform. "We must not forget that I am President of the whole country, not of any party," said Hayes. Cooperation could not come at the price of reform.[11]

The impasse lasted until January 1879, when a White House secretary appeared at the doors of the Senate with what one observer called "a wheelbarrow load of documents," more than enough to convince a majority of senators that Hayes did not exaggerate the odor of corruption permeating the New York Custom House under the elegant grafter Chester Arthur. Arthur was removed. As news of his triumph circulated, the abstemious Hayes was said to be in a jubilant frame of mind. According to one reporter, "The water flowed like Champagne."[12]

No less committed to the reform agenda was the first lady. Lightning may or may not strike twice, but that is no reason to conclude that history never repeats itself. If you doubt that, consider a polarizing woman deemed by her critics to be overeducated, excessively opinionated, and far too influential in her unelected position. A strong-willed social reformer and deft political operator, she made no attempt to conceal her fiery opinions, and for all her attention to the social amenities—whether inaugurating the White House Easter Egg Roll or launching a short-lived fad with her ornamental hair combs—her real objective was nothing less than to redefine traditional women's roles in America.

Her name was Lucy Webb Hayes. And far from the prudish "Lemonade Lucy" of popular legend, Mrs. Rutherford B. Hayes was a feminist heroine, the most popular, and reviled, first lady until Eleanor Roosevelt. "Woman's mind is as strong as man's," she insisted, "equal in all things and his superior in some."[13] She came by her views as the latest in a long line of reformers, equally fervent in their advocacy of public education, temperance, and the abolition of slavery. She also developed an early, very unladylike interest in politics. Despite giving birth to eight children in twenty years, Lucy maintained a lively interest in public affairs. As the wife of Ohio's governor, she visited state prisons and mental hospitals; she also raised funds with which to construct a facility for war orphans. Banishing the White House bil-

Lucy Webb Hayes in the Conservatory at the White House with Scott and Fanny, two of her children, and Carrie Davis, a friend, 1879.

liard table to the basement, Mrs. Hayes held daily prayer meetings and weekly hymn singing, the latter featuring the first lady's rich contralto as well as the booming bass of Vice President William Wheeler.

Her far-flung campaign for temperance won Lucy millions of fans, and more than a few detractors. Sniffed the *Boston Post,* "Mr. Hayes will, during the absence of Mrs. Hayes, be acting President."[14] Undeterred, the first lady looked the other way when a saloon christening itself "The Last Chance" opened its doors a stone's throw from the White House. Her confidence was well placed. "Mrs. Hayes may not have much influence with the Senate," said her husband, "but she has a great deal with me."[15] This was publicly displayed every Sunday morning. Himself a disciple of Ralph Waldo Emerson, President Hayes attended church services mostly to please his devout wife. Once invited to name his sectarian preferences, Hayes puckishly declared his closeness to Methodism, since he slept every night with one of that persuasion.

There were, however, limits, even to his good nature. When the Hayeses observed their twenty-fifth wedding anniversary in the White House, Lucy's brother Joseph was notably absent from the festivities. The president's brother-in-law boycotted the event after Hayes refused to bend his rule against nepotism and give him a government job. The Senate, unlike Joseph, was in a position to exact revenge, even against the first lady and her domestic arrangements. Denied adequate funding with which to refurbish the shabby old house, Lucy took to rearranging furniture to cover the worst holes in threadbare White House rugs. Dipping into her husband's private fortune, she entertained lavishly. The menu for one such occasion—the bill for which could run as high as $2,400—provides abundant evidence of why this period of White House history might be christened the Age of Excess.

As recounted by Hayes's biographer Ari Hoogenboom, diplomatic representatives were treated to a repast of "Salmon à la Vatrelle, sauce à la Ravigotte, boned turkey and truffles, game patés and truffles, ham glacé, filet de volaille à la Carlette, chicken salads, lobster salads, oyster patés, scalloped oysters, chicken croquet on truffles, terrapin (diamond back), sandwiches, tea, coffee, and chocolate." On the White House dessert tables sat "Meringues baskets, Newgate pyramids, Charlotte russe jellies, water ices, and candied fruit, plus the notorious oranges," the notoriety of the last stemming from reports that a White House steward had taken to injecting oranges with Santa Croix rum.[16] Only after leaving office did Hayes reveal the joke: he had personally directed their flavoring with a rumlike substitute that hadn't a drop of spirits in it. Presiding over this splendid scene was a regal hostess, described by the normally acerbic Mrs. Henry Adams as "quite nice looking, dark with smooth black hair combed low over the ears and a high comb behind—her dress a plain untrimmed black silk, a broad white Smyrna lace tie around her neck—no jewelry." Clover Adams was decidedly less complimentary on the subject of the Hayeses' gift to the White House, an artistically stunning set of Haviland china that realistically portrayed American flora and fauna. It was impossible to eat one's soup in a calm frame of mind, claimed Mrs. Adams, "with a coyote springing at you."[17]

Like millions of American households in those feverish years, the Hayes White House sought to balance material progress with cultural and spiritual ferment. That is hardly its only parallel with our own era of flagrant display and accelerating change. From time to time, overwrought journalists proclaim us to be inhabitants of a new Gilded Age. We should be so lucky. Between 1865 and 1900 the rate of illiteracy in America was cut in half. Expenditures on education tripled. College enrollment soared by 700 percent, with Lucy Hayes becoming the first president's wife to have attended college. Within the span of a few protean years, Lucy's countrymen witnessed the debut of open-hearth steel manufacturing, the air brake and sleeping car, frozen food, the photographic sky plate, and Chicago's Union Stockyards. A nation without telephones in 1876 counted 1.5 million of the devices in use by the end of the century. Hayes himself had the first White House phone—inevitably bearing the number 1—installed in 1879. On another occasion Thomas Edison kept the first couple up until 3:30 A.M. with a demonstration of his new talking box, or phonograph. Soon after, Hayes was persuaded to order from Fairbanks and Company its improved Number Two Typewriter—the first machine of its kind to alleviate secretarial chores for the small executive staff.

As life sped up, it was inevitable that some cast longing eyes over their shoulders. Hard on the heels of the nation's centennial, Lucretia Garfield became the first White House occupant to conduct serious research into the history of the house. Mrs. Garfield also hired seven people to form what she called the Bureau of Apartments. The Garfields reversed social if not political course, receiving a portrait of Lemonade Lucy from the Woman's Christian Temperance Union while simultaneously opening cellars full of Grant's well-aged wine. The new president also accepted the loan of Hayes's elegant carriage. Less welcome was the unending procession of office-seekers who infested the second floor staircase and accosted the president on Washington's streets. "These people would take my very brain, flesh and blood if they could," Garfield muttered.[18]

In this Garfield proved tragically prophetic. In the summer of 1881 a group of navy engineers was summoned to the White House, where the president lay in an-

James A. Garfield.

guish following the attempt on his life by a disappointed office-seeker and author, who had hoped by shooting the nation's chief executive to promote the sales of his book (thereby reversing the modern order in which killers wait until after their crime to cash in). Not for the first time in the Gilded Age, necessity mothered invention, as desperate navy men improvised the world's first air conditioner, using a concept put forth by one R. S. Jennings of Baltimore. This consisted of a blower that forced air cooled by six tons of ice through a heat vent in the president's sickroom, thereby lowering the temperature by some twenty degrees. The patient remained snappish—hardly surprising, given his diet of oatmeal and lime water. On learning that the Indian warrior Sitting Bull was starving in captivity, Garfield snorted, "Let him starve." Then, a still more wicked alternative suggested itself to the dying president: "Send him my oatmeal," said Garfield.[19]

Less successful than the jerry-built air conditioner was Alexander Graham Bell's metal detector. Brought into Garfield's second-floor bedroom, the device mistakenly indicated a bullet lodged in the president's right groin. This and other medical errors led Garfield's assailant, Charles J. Guiteau, to brazenly disclaim responsibility for his victim's death. Said Guiteau, "The doctors did that. I simply shot him."[20]

When the end came for Garfield, on September 15, 1881, it was at a seaside cottage near Long Beach, New Jersey, to which the dying chief executive had been moved in the hope that ocean breezes might reverse his decline. Garfield's successor, Chester Arthur, refused to accept a bodyguard. He did, however, insist on the services of a valet, which was only appropriate for the so-called Dude President, who was said to own eighty pairs of shoes and an extensive wardrobe. True to form, Garfield's successor Arthur refused to move into that "badly kept barracks," the White House, pending extensive renovations. Twenty-four wagon loads of hair mattresses, marble mantels, and cuspidors were hauled off to auction. These gave way to a robin's egg blue color scheme, fashioned by Louis C. Tiffany, as well as the first tiled bathroom in White House history.

Arthur the connoisseur became equally famous for the cut of his clothes, the quality of his food, and the warmth of his manner. The music-loving president welcomed Adelina Patti and Christine Nilsson to the East Room. More moving than either was a February 1882 concert by the Fisk Jubilee Singers. Arthur's first state dinner, given in honor of former President and Mrs. Grant, set the tone for what followed. It consisted of fourteen courses, accompanied by eight varieties of wine. An equally lavish event featured "the Swinging Garden of Babylon," a four-foot-long floral centerpiece composed of roses, honeysuckle, and red and white carnations. The persnickety Mrs. James G. Blaine, only too glad to be liberated from Lucy's arid entertainments, was predictably impressed. "I dined at the president's Wednesday," she wrote. "The dinner was extremely elegant, hardly a trace of the old White House taint being perceptible anywhere, the flowers, the damask, the silver, the attendance, all showing the latest style and an abandon in expense and taste."[21]

From former President Hayes came no such praise. "Nothing like it ever before in the Executive Mansion," Hayes complained to his diary, "liquor, snobbery, and worse."[22] Diagnosed with Bright's disease, a fatal kidney ailment, Arthur kept his condition more or less secret, thereby inspiring fresh criticism of a pleasure-loving chief executive. The president's lack of interest in paperwork prompted one staff member to observe that "President Arthur never did today what he could put off until tomorrow."[23] On the other hand, Arthur was no more successful than his murdered predecessor in escaping the crush of office-seekers. Soon the harried president was arguing for a physical separation between executive offices and the private residence. "You have no idea how depressing and fatiguing it is to live in the same house where you work," Arthur told one reporter. "The downtown businessman in New York would feel quite differently if after the close of his day he were to sit down in the atmosphere of his office to find rest and recreation instead of going uptown to cut loose absolutely from everything connected with his work of the day."[24]

Thus began the agitation for an entirely new White House, a movement that would reach its peak under Mrs. Benjamin Harrison and limited realization under Edith Roosevelt early in the twentieth century. As the republic came of age, it cautiously dipped a toe in foreign waters. Newly literate consumers of mass journals demanded a more personalized presidency. Yet the White House remained a bastion of reticence. To Gilded Age presidents, the fourth estate was at best a fifth wheel. Not only did Arthur conceal his illness from prying eyes; he managed to hide his domestic life generally. For this he was applauded by traditionalists. Wrote one self-proclaimed arbiter of the Arthur administration, "Coarse-minded, peeping correspondents, male and female, found scant material here from vulgar paragraphs of kitchen gossip. There were published no foolish, nauseating chronicles of the 'daily doings' of the White House. The president's children were not photographed and paragraphed and made the subject of a thousand flat and fatuous stories. Beyond the veil of self-respecting privacy, which was drawn before the president's personal affairs, few ever penetrated."[25]

Arthur's successors were to be less fortunate. During the last quarter of the nineteenth century, when the number of American newspapers quadrupled, the

Entrance Hall, ca. 1890, showing the Tiffany colored-glass screen. A glass screen had been here since 1837, when central heating was installed. Tiffany improved it in 1882 by replacing the ordinary ground glass with colored glass in murky tones of red, white, and blue. Photograph by Frances Benjamin Johnston.

man in the White House and his family became a vivid presence in people's lives, whether they liked it or not. Mostly they did not. Even earlier an angry Ulysses S. Grant had declared, "I have been the subject of abuse and slander scarcely ever equaled in political history." Grant's lament would grow familiar with repetition. Miraculously Grover Cleveland kept secret his June 1893 cancer operation, which unfolded on board a yacht in New York harbor. Not so the instant celebrity visited upon Cleveland's daughter Ruth, whose imaginary link to the Baby Ruth candy bar remains, a century later, her chief claim to posterity's notice.[26]

The news wasn't the only thing to be democratized. The struggle for sexual equality advanced in tandem with economic and political innovations. When it comes to the conventional view of Victorian women, especially political women, as mere ornaments, the Gilded Age White House affords abundant evidence to buttress what Dame Veronica Wedgwood called "the delightful undermining of certainty." The much-abused Grant had appointed five thousand female postmasters. This was enough to earn Susan B. Anthony's illegal vote but not, it seems, her gratitude. The urbane Chester Arthur welcomed Miss Anthony and a delegation of female suffragists, one of them dressed for the occasion in a man's frock coat and a high silk hat. Grover Cleveland's sister Rose, herself an accomplished scholar, confided to a friend that the only way she managed to survive brain-numbing White House reception lines was by conjugating Greek verbs while shaking hands.[27]

Rose could relax after June 1886, when her forty-nine-year-old brother wed twenty-one-year-old Frances Folsom, the daughter of Cleveland's law partner. (In her youth Miss Folsom had called him "Uncle Cleve.") John Philip Sousa's red-jacketed Marine Band serenaded the couple as they appeared in the Blue Room. Decidedly less welcome were reporters equipped with spyglasses and cameras, forerunners of today's paparazzi, who pursued the newlyweds to a Maryland mountain resort in search of yet another kind of gold: the scoop relentlessly sought by the Pulitzers and Hearsts, for whom sensation paved the low road to riches and political power of their own. It was not the first time Cleveland had confronted peephole journalists. In his 1884 campaign against Republican James G. Blaine, the Democratic contender had manfully acknowledged fathering a child—instantly dubbed "Little Tom Tid" by an enterprising songwriter—out of wedlock.

Cleveland was far less compliant when it came to this latest intrusion on his, and his bride's, privacy. "They have used the enormous power of the modern newspaper to perpetuate and disseminate a colossal impertinence," the president raged, "and have done it, not as professional gossips and tattlers, but as the guides and instructors of the public in conduct and morals. And they have done it, not to a private citizen, but the President of the United States, thereby lifting their offence into the gaze of the whole world, and doing their utmost to make American journalism contemptible in the estimation of people of good breeding everywhere."[28]

So much for the conceit of trash-for-cash journalism as a modern invention. Never mind: Frances was an instant media star. Women copied her hairstyle. Her picture appeared on commercial advertisements, not always with her consent. The president adored his young bride; late one night he was spotted by a servant moving her noisome mockingbird to a room where it wouldn't interrupt his labors, or

Detail of a gold-leafed chair by Herter Brothers, New York, purchased by Julia Dent Grant for the Red Room in 1875 (see page 72).

catch a chill. He also let Frances talk him out of wearing an orange suit of which he was uncommonly, if inexplicably, proud. (The first lady said it might cost him the Irish vote.) On a slow news day, unscrupulous journalists made up a story that Frances would discard her imprisoning bustle. During a nasty reelection campaign in 1888, she was forced to deny rumors that her husband beat her. In time bothersome reporters drove the Clevelands to take up residence for several months each year at a suburban retreat they named Oak View, and a noncooperative press insisted on calling it Red Top.

Frances Cleveland's successor, Caroline Lavinia Harrison, had her own problems with unwanted commercial exploitation. An unflattering likeness of Mrs. Harrison was used to sell girdle fasteners. The daughter of a Presbyterian minister who strongly supported education for women, Caroline raised funds for the Johns Hopkins Medical School, on condition that it be coeducational. She also served as first president general of the Daughters of the American Revolution. On the home front, the first lady confronted appalling conditions. Inadequate plumbing had caused green mold to form on White House walls. Rotting floorboards, in some places five layers deep, crawled with vermin. At one point early in her husband's term, Mrs. Harrison actually fell ill from escaping sewer gas.

The Harrison administration produced a milestone of sorts in the form of the nation's first billion-dollar budget. (Tasked with extravagance, Speaker of the House Tom Reed professed unconcern, asserting that the United States had gotten to be a billion-dollar country.) Arthur's plans for an expanded White House were resuscitated on an even grander scale. What came to be known as Mrs. Harrison's Model envisioned round pavilions added to the existing mansion. Separate wings devoted to art and office space would frame a square dominated by a giant "Allegorical Fountain." Speaker Reed killed the project in a dispute over patronage, forcing Caroline Harrison to settle for newly installed electric lights and a porcelain-lined bathtub that, according to her husband, "would tempt a duck to wash himself everyday."[29]

A true conservative, the president shied away from contact with electric lights in the hallways and public rooms out of fear he might be electrocuted. According to Ike Hoover, the longtime usher whose first job was to oversee the mansion's wiring, the Harrisons even hesitated before using electric-powered buttons to summon servants.[30] Other innovations were more welcome. Dancing returned to the White House for the first time since the Grant era. A gifted artist, Mrs. Harrison designed her own striking pattern of official china. The first lady provided heirlooms by the hundreds for mothers who named their infants after the presi-

White House china from President Benjamin Harrison's administration. By law, American manufacturers have to be given first consideration when the White House buys; although this Limoges dinnerware was of French manufacture, it was acceptable because it was purchased through an agency in the United States.

dent. When not painting milk sets and pitchers, she was busy adorning candlesticks, cracker boxes, and cheese covers. Besides conducting classes in china painting, supplemented by French lessons for cabinet wives and daughters, she initiated the public display of historic china from earlier administrations.

It would take more than painted china to humanize Caroline's husband. Inevitably, a press corps looking for mass appeal zeroed in on the Harrison's irrepressible grandson, "Baby McKee." The child's antics included driving a goat cart into Pennsylvania Avenue, followed in hot pursuit by the president of the United States in top hat and frock coat. Then, as later, media attention threatened to get out of hand. One party regular went so far as to compose a popular verse linking

Vice President Levi Morton, whose Shoreham Hotel featured a well-attended bar, and the Bible-toting postmaster general, John P. Wanamaker:

> *The baby runs the White House;*
> *Levi runs the bar;*
> *Wanny runs the Sunday School,*
> *And, damn it, here we are.*[31]

Office-seekers were indeed there, where they had always been, the bane of presidential existence. Driven to distraction by one tiresome petitioner, Harrison assured his caller, "I grasp the situation." "That's just the trouble," said the would-be postmaster. "What I want is for you to let go of the situation so that I can grasp it."[32] The appetite for power, only slightly curbed by the passage of civil service reform legislation, would outlast the ebbing Gilded Age.

Caroline Harrison died in the closing weeks of her husband's unsuccessful 1892 bid for reelection. The future was embodied in Harrison's bumptious civil service commissioner, Theodore Roosevelt, who would, before a decade had passed, banish the potted ferns and velvet fringe of the old house in favor of a severely elegant federal style appropriate to the eighteenth century—or the twentieth. In the new order journalists laid claim to quarters in the temporary west wing built by TR in belated recognition of Arthur's lament and Caroline Harrison's vision.

In other ways did the vigorous new president, the nation's youngest, hearken back to an earlier time. Roosevelt's namesake father had been at the center of Hayes's crusade to scour the notorious New York Custom House; it was Hayes's failure to replace Arthur with the first Theodore Roosevelt that had marked a turning point in his battle with the Senate over civil service reform. And what of Lucy and Rud? In March 1881 they had returned to Spiegel Grove, their beloved estate near Fremont, Ohio. The former president joined the Peabody Educational Fund, taking a special interest in the education of African Americans in the South. Emulating Lucy's outspokenness, Hayes became more unguarded in his comments, especially when dealing with the undue concentration of wealth. He made no secret of his fear that excessive fortunes would undermine economic and social democracy. For ten years Hayes served as president of the National Prison Association. Someone asked why he lent his name to the cause of prison reform. "We prefer to give special attention to the unpopular questions," said Hayes, "to those that need friends."[33]

In June 1889 Hayes lost his greatest friend when Lucy suffered a stroke in her

This model was made by the Army Corps of Engineers in 1900 as a means of selling the idea of a greatly expanded White House to President William McKinley and the American people. The enlargement was meant to celebrate the one hundredth anniversary of John Adams's move to the White House.

bedroom at Spiegel Grove. "She is in heaven," wrote a grieving husband. "She is where all the best of earth have gone."[34] On the morning of Sunday, January 8, 1893, Hayes went to visit Lucy's grave in the local cemetery. That evening he wrote in his diary of his longing to join her. At the Cleveland train station a few days later he experienced severe chest pains. "I would rather die at Spiegel Grove," he told onlookers, "than to live anywhere else."[35] On the night of January 17 his wish was granted. President-elect Grover Cleveland made the long train journey from Washington to attend his predecessor's funeral. "He was coming to see me," explained Cleveland. "But he is dead and I will go to him."[36]

The gesture would have touched Hayes. For by his simple gallantry, Cleveland buried all the old charges about the disputed election of 1876, along with the man who had won it. His Fraudulency, long since relegated to memory, was replaced by Hayes the Reconciler. Not long before his death, Hayes observed to a friend that his marriage to Lucy Webb had been the most interesting fact of his life. It is a sentiment from which few White House historians would dissent. More than a century later, Rud and Lucy—especially Lucy—remain the true gold in the Gilded Age.

WHITE HOUSE COLLECTION

NOTES

1. Justin Kaplan, *Mr. Clemens and Mark Twain* (New York: Simon and Schuster, 1966), 96; see also Paul Boller, *Presidential Anecdotes* (New York: Penguin Books, 1981), 165. Twain was careful to add that, in his opinion, "the present era of incredible rottenness is not Democratic, it is not Republican, it is *national*." Walt Whitman also chose 1871 to publish his own lament for postwar America in his book *Democratic Vistas* (reprint; New York: Liberal Arts Press, 1949), 40. "America, if eligible at all to downfall and ruin, is eligible within herself, not without; for I see clearly that the combined foreign world could not beat her down. But these savage, wolfish parties alarm me."

2. Thomas Wolfe, *From Death to Morning* (New York: Charles Scribner's Sons, 1935), 121. Little in the American historical canon is so fixed as the relentlessly mediocre image of the White House's post–Civil War occupants. "Never before or since has the Presidency counted for so little as it did in the last three decades of the nineteenth century," writes Hugh Brogan in *The Penguin History of the U.S.A.* (New York: Penguin Books, 1990), 419. To Page Smith, presidents from Hayes through McKinley were "forgettable" at best. Henry Adams broadened the historical indictment to include the postwar era, claiming that "no period so thoroughly ordinary had been known in American politics since Christopher Columbus first disturbed the balance of American society" (George Brown Tindall, *America: A Narrative History* [New York: W. W. Norton, 1984], 2:825). It is a criticism echoed by New Deal historians, for whom the great crime of most nineteenth-century presidents is their failure to act like most twentieth-century presidents.

3. Quoted in Charles King, *The True Ulysses S. Grant* (Philadelphia: J. B. Lippincott, 1914), 313–14.

4. Quoted in Gore Vidal, *United States: Essays: 1952–1992* (New York: Random House, 1993), 721.

5. Julia Dent Grant, *The Personal Memoirs of Julia Dent Grant,* ed. John Y. Simon (Carbondale and Edwardsville: Southern Illinois University Press, 1975), 174–75.

6. Richard Goldhurst, *Many Are the Hearts* (New York: Reader's Digest Press, 1975), 94.

7. Standard accounts of the Gilded Age presidency accuse Thomas Wolfe's "Lost Americans" of timidity. It would be more accurate to say that these soldier-politicians regarded the Constitution as a limiting, rather than an enabling, document. Grant, in particular, has been condemned for permitting white supremacists in the South to snatch racial victory from the jaws of military defeat. More recently, however, Reconstruction-era historians such as Ari Hoogenboom and Brooks Sampson, as well as Grant biographers Jean Edward Smith and Frank J. Scaturro, have forcefully argued that Grant did more than any other political leader of the period to enforce civil rights laws, combat terrorist groups like the Ku Klux Klan, and extend the protections guaranteed by the Fourteenth and Fifteenth Amendments throughout a resistant South. At the same time, those scholars have called into question the conventional picture of Grant-era corruption, pointing out that scandals like the Crédit Mobilier had roots in earlier administrations, disputing the guilt of presidential subordinates (Secretary of War William Belknap notably excepted), and crediting the president with the first steps toward civil service reform.

8. Henry Adams, *The Education of Henry Adams* (1907; reprint, New York: Modern Library, 1999), 261. What Henry Adams mordantly labeled his education was in reality the disillusionment of one who wanted nothing more than a career in which social position had value. He was hardly alone. Taking their cue from Alexis de Tocqueville, who had advocated an intellectual aristocracy in place of hereditary privilege, a reformist guild of clergymen, philanthropists, college professors, social and other scientists, authors, and editorial writers hoped, with Adams, to redeem their country and their class. Among their ranks was Theodore Roosevelt, senior, another high-minded reformer who was not above hiring a mercenary to fight for him in the Civil War. Roosevelt's embarrassed namesake would spend a lifetime compensating for his father's action. Subtle as a Thomas Nast cartoon, his noisy saber rattling in 1898 coincided with America's next great surge of missionary spirit, as the sons of Union and Confederate veterans together fought an imperial war with decrepit Spain to Christianize and Americanize the world. TR the romantic would, in time, denounce the years between Appomattox and San Juan Hill as "a riot of individual materialism . . . turned out in practice to mean perfect freedom for the strong to wrong the weak." Thus, the fruits of unregulated competition contained the seeds of Progressive-era trust-busting.

9. Harry Barnard, *Rutherford B. Hayes and His America* (Indianapolis: Bobbs-Merrill 1954), ix.

10. Henry Adams, *Education,* 261.

11. Quoted in Thomas C. Reeves, *Gentleman Boss: The Life of Chester Alan Arthur* (New York: Alfred A. Knopf, 1975), 127.

12. George F. Hoar, *Autobiography of Seventy Years* (New York: Charles Scribner's Sons, 1906) 2:15.

13. Of particular interest to students of Lucy Webb Hayes is Cheryl Heckler-Feltz, "A Strong Lady in the White House," *Ohio Magazine* 19, no. 6 (October 1996): 18–21; 58. To this day, it is er-

roneously believed that it was Lucy, and not her abstemious husband, behind the ban on alcohol at White House functions. To be sure, on Washington's Birthday, 1878, President Hayes solemnly reviewed the "Cold Water Army" of prohibitionists as it passed the White House. Yet both Hayeses dismayed hard-shell abstainers that spring when they permitted a claret punch to be served in their presence at a Philadelphia dinner. The Lucy Hayes Temperance Society of Washington angrily changed its name. According to Heckler-Feltz, Lucy's sensitivity toward her numerous friends of German-American heritage prompted her moderate approach. Whatever the cause, it was enough to inspire Mark Twain's celebrated jest: "Total Abstinence is so excellent a thing that it cannot be carried to too great an extreme. In my passion for it, I even carry it so far as to totally abstain from Total Abstinence itself." "Mark Twain Tonight," CBS broadcast, March 6, 1967.

14. Quoted in H. J. Eckenrode, *Rutherford B. Hayes: Statesman of Reunion* (New York: Dodd, Mead, 1930), 312.

15. Heckler-Feltz, "Strong Lady."

16. Ari Hoogenboom, *Rutherford B. Hayes: Warrior and President* (Lawrence: University Press of Kansas, 1995), 386.

17. Quoted ibid., 348, 462.

18. Glen Paskin, *Garfield* (Kent, Ohio: Kent State University Press, 1978), 551.

19. Ibid., 601.

20. Ibid., 603.

21. Quoted in Reeves, *Gentleman Boss,* 270–71.

22. Hayes's diary entry is quoted in Eckenrode, *Rutherford B. Hayes,* 335.

23. Quoted in Reeves, *Gentleman Boss,* 273.

24. Quoted ibid., 274.

25. Marcus Cunliffe, *The American Heritage History of the Presidency* (New York: American Heritage, 1968), 202.

26. The story of Grover Cleveland's illness and subsequent cover-up is told by Allan Nevins, *Grover Cleveland: A Study in Courage* (New York: Dodd, Mead, 1932), 2:528–31; Alyn Brodsky, *Grover Cleveland: A Study in Character* (New York: St. Martin's Press, 2000), 310–16.

27. *Madame President: America's First Ladies* (Simi Valley, Calif.: Ronald Reagan Presidential Library, 1994), 24.

28. Quoted in Brodsky, *Grover Cleveland,* 174. Needless to say, Cleveland's complaints about "that dirty gang" of reporters have been echoed by virtually every American chief executive since.

29. Harry J. Sievers, *Benjamin Harrison: Hoosier President* (Indianapolis: Bobbs-Merrill, 1968), 94.

30. Ike Hoover quoted ibid., 94.

31. Sievers, *Benjamin Harrison,* 56.

32. Quoted in George S. Hilton, *The Funny Side of Politics* (New York: G. W. Dillingham, 1899), 192.

33. Quoted in Barnard, *Rutherford B. Hayes,* 507.

34. Ibid., 511.

35. Quoted in Hoogenboom, *Rutherford B. Hayes,* 532.

36. Quoted in Nevins, *Grover Cleveland,* 2:563.

Frances Benjamin Johnston sets up her camera—probably the 8x10 view camera produced for her by George Eastman—on the terrace of the State, War and Navy Building west of the White House, 1888.

Chapter 7

Frances Benjamin Johnston's White House

WILLIAM B. BUSHONG

Described as a "tall graceful blond of cultivated manners, dignified carriage, and tasteful dress," photographer Frances B. Johnston (1864–1952) in public looked the part of the conventional professional businesswoman.[1] Yet, as her famous self-portrait with a raised skirt and beer stein and cigarette in hand showed, she was independent minded and had a bohemian streak. Johnston, who studied art in Paris between 1883 and 1885 at the Académie Julian, returned to Washington, D.C., to become a leading member of the arts community and the beloved hostess of "the Push," a band of Washington artists who frequented her studio. About 1887 she wrote to George Eastman, possibly a family friend, and asked him to send a camera. She planned to experiment with the medium and ended up working as an agent for Eastman for several years. In 1890 she took advanced photographic training under Thomas William Smillie, the Smithsonian Institution's first curator of photography. After two decades as a freelance photographer in Washington, Johnston moved on to New York City in 1909 to specialize in architectural and garden photography. The culmination of her career came with the Carnegie Corporation's support of a major architectural survey of the early buildings and estates of nine southern states in the 1930s. She settled in the South and died in New Orleans in 1952.

Johnston blended commercial and artistic sensibilities to become one of the most successful and prominent photographers of her time. Her documentary work, including the photographic series for the District of Columbia public schools, the Hampton Institute, the Carlisle Indian School, and the Tuskegee Institute between 1899 and 1906, was considered exemplary and helped establish her reputation as a master American photographer. However, her work in Washington, D.C., from about 1888 to 1909, though less well known, was also remarkable. She

97

The East Room. Architecturally the room is as Ulysses S. Grant remodeled it in 1874 for his daughter Nellie's wedding. The picture of Dolley Madison was an intended mate to the well-known one of Martha Washington in the East Room today, both painted by E. F. Andrews of the Corcoran Gallery of Art. Although much effort was made to coax the government into buying this painting, the sale was never made, and it has hung for a century in the Cosmos Club in Washington. Photograph by Frances Benjamin Johnston, 1893.

captured striking images of the people and the cityscape of the nation's capital and emerged in the 1890s as America's court photographer.

Johnston's photographs of the White House in the later Gilded Age form a significant chapter in her career during a period that was dominated by work in photojournalism and portraiture. It is not known exactly how Johnston gained access at the White House, but her papers suggest she cultivated friendships with both the first families and the staff. About 1893 Johnston established an important association with George Grantham Bain, an influential New York picture agent. Johnston's papers in the 1890s are filled with notes and telegrams from Bain requesting images to accompany news stories about the White House, the first family, the president, and members of the cabinet. Johnston obliged and, through Bain, provided news and family magazines with a steady supply of images of the first family, the White House building, its staff at work, and events that ranged from the annual Easter Egg Roll to presidential receptions.

Johnston's architectural photography in this period, much of which was commissioned for use in newspapers, magazines, and books, was also noteworthy. It has been overshadowed by the approximately 7,500 negatives that she produced later in life for the great Carnegie survey of southern architecture. However, her architectural education and appreciation of historic buildings must have been inspired in Washington as she extensively photographed the White House, the U.S. Capitol, and many other public buildings, parks, and houses. In the 1890s she collaborated closely with the Washington architect Glenn Brown, a leader in the colonial revival movement in the city and a pioneering architectural historian. Johnston illustrated Brown's numerous articles on the historic L'Enfant plan of Washington, the domestic architecture of the city, and public architecture. Their collaboration culminated in the publication of hundreds of plates of interior and exterior views of the Capitol taken between 1893 and 1900 and copy work of historic drawings and documents to illustrate Brown's two-volume *History of the United States Capitol*.

Ironically, many of Johnston's earliest images of White House interiors shot

LIBRARY OF CONGRESS

Frances Benjamin Johnston, perhaps a self-portrait, 1903.

Frances Folsom Cleveland seated in the West Sitting Hall upstairs at the White House about 1888, toward the end of her husband's first term. Photograph by Frances Benjamin Johnston.

between 1889 and 1893 were used by Brown and other government fine arts re-formers to argue for and then to defend the Beaux Arts makeover of the White House at the turn of the century. These photographs became the "before" images characterized by supporters of McKim, Mead & White's 1902 renovation work as Gilded Age illustrations of a "dark age of art history."[2]

Prior to 1900 Frances Benjamin Johnston already had created a significant body of White House photographs. She was the first photographer to document the house extensively in the nineteenth century. Yet these photographs were only a portion of her White House portfolio built over two decades. Johnston's collection, which she donated to the Library of Congress, included hundreds of invaluable photographs taken from the Cleveland through the Taft administrations. She

Rows of carriages await their passengers, who are inside at President Grover Cleveland's 1889 New Year's reception. Frances Benjamin Johnston's camera captured one of the glamorous traditional events of the White House, carried on from its inception until 1932, when the logistics of greeting so many people became too complicated. An average crowd for a New Year's reception was six thousand.

recorded the White House as a work space and a seat of power and documented the house's appearance at a time when its interior architectural design and functional character changed dramatically. Her legacy in creating the public image of the Gilded Age White House was powerful and today continues to influence our perception of the past of the house.[3]

Jerry Smith, a butler in the 1890s, began his White House career as a stableman, then was a footman for Mrs. Grant, Mrs. Hayes, Mrs. Garfield, and Mrs. Cleveland, and at last became part of the domestic staff, where he remained for many years. Photograph by Frances Benjamin Johnston, ca. 1890.

LIBRARY OF CONGRESS

William McKinley and his cabinet in the Cabinet Room, on the second floor, today known as the Treaty Room. Photograph by Frances Benjamin Johnston, ca. 1898.

NOTES

1. C. D. Arnold to Frances Benjamin Johnston, June 5, 1892, Johnston Papers, Library of Congress.

2. Glenn Brown, "The New White House," *Harper's Weekly,* July 14, 1906, 989.

3. For further reading, see Frances Benjamin Johnston Papers, Manuscript Division, Library of Congress, Washington, D.C.; Frances Benjamin Johnston Collection, Prints and Photographs Division, Library of Congress, Washington, D.C.; Pete Daniel and Raymond Smock, *A Talent for Detail: The Photographs of Miss Frances Benjamin Johnston, 1889–1910* (New York: Harmony Books, 1974); Bettina Berch, *The Woman Behind the Lens: The Life and Work of Frances Benjamin Johnston, 1864–1952* (Charlottesville: University Press of Virginia, 2000; William B. Bushong, "Glenn Brown, the American Institute of Architects, and the Development of the Civic Core of Washington, D.C.," Ph.D. diss., George Washington University, 1988.

At President McKinley's request, the signing of the peace protocol to end the hostilities between Spain and the United States was held in his office and Cabinet Room on August 12, 1898. By special arrangement, the original participants returned on August 20 and recreated the scene for a photograph taken by Frances Benjamin Johnston. President McKinley stood at the center, surrounded by members of the diplomatic community and members of his office staff, while Secretary of State William Day signed the document for the United States. According to the Johnston papers at the Library of Congress, Adjutant-General of the U.S. Army H. C. Corbin, standing third from left, was not one of the original witnesses but was calling on the president on August 20 and invited to join the group. Johnston also took a photograph showing French Ambassador Jules Cambon signing the document on behalf of Spain.

Images of the White House, 1890–1910

LYDIA BARKER TEDERICK

L IFE at the White House at the turn of the twentieth century was well documented by photographers. Numerous photographs were taken not only of the exterior and interior of the White House but of presidential families in the public and the private areas of the residence. In addition, although not as numerous, photographs were made of the office staff upstairs in their working environments.

A major reason for this abundance of images was the increased popularity of stereographs. Firms such as Underwood & Underwood and Keystone View Company dramatically escalated the publishing of stereographs during the late 1800s and early 1900s. The administrations of William McKinley and Theodore Roosevelt, including their party conventions and inaugurations, were extensively photographed by stereo photographers working for these two companies and for other, smaller publishers.[1]

Frances Benjamin Johnston, who had photographed the White House and presidential families during the Cleveland and Harrison administrations, was again granted access to document the McKinley White House. Several of her photographs show both William and Ida McKinley in various White House settings. Her photographs also record the executive office and its staff during the Spanish-American War.

Prior to 1902, the executive office comprised a few rooms at the east end of the second floor of the White House. The family quarters occupied the remainder of this floor. Rooms originally intended for domestic use were adapted for business, and they looked like what they were, converted bedchambers and dressing rooms.[2] These rooms are today used as the principal guest rooms and are known as the Queens' Bedroom, the Queens' Sitting Room, the Lincoln Bedroom, and the

President William McKinley's staff office in the east end of the second floor of the White House. Crowded into five rooms and a central hall, the presidential offices were close quarters; the intrusion of innovation made them even tighter. Everyone knew there should be a better office situation, but no one had time to create it. Photograph by Frances Benjamin Johnston, ca. 1898.

William McKinley's coffin in state in the East Room, September 1901, prior to his funeral at the Capitol.

Kermit Roosevelt poses with his terrier, Jack. Photograph by Frances Benjamin Johnston, 1902.

Quentin and Archie Roosevelt play with Frances Benjamin Johnston's camera at the White House, 1902.

Lincoln Sitting Room. The nineteenth-century Cabinet Room has been used as a study by twentieth-century presidents and is called the Treaty Room.

The overcrowded conditions of the office area were magnified during the Spanish-American War. There were no facilities for reporters. Telephones were not made available to them, and they were asked not to use the waiting room—itself an adapted corridor—as a lounge. When they got news, the journalists ran their stories downstairs to messengers on bicycles or horseback, who raced to the telegraph office to wire the text to their respective newspapers.[3]

As stereo photographers covered President McKinley's inauguration, they also

The wedding of President Roosevelt's oldest daughter, Alice Lee Roosevelt, to Ohio Congressman Nicholas Longworth was held in the East Room on February 17, 1906. It was a social event of international interest. A staid official photograph, taken by Edward S. Curtis, was posed in a setting using an antique Flemish tapestry from the State Dining Room, apparently arranged around a platform. A certain likeness between father and groom did not go unnoticed at the time.

The new Executive Office Building near completion in this construction photograph of what would one day develop into the West Wing. The remains of the great conservatories can still be seen, as the White House building project for Theodore Roosevelt comes to an end. Photograph by Frances Benjamin Johnston, 1902.

covered his funeral. While visiting the Pan-American Exposition in Buffalo, New York, on September 6, 1901, six months after his second inauguration, the president was shot and fatally wounded by a self-proclaimed anarchist, Leon F. Czolgosz.[4] The president died in Buffalo on September 14. His body was returned to the White House and lay in state in the East Room.

Upon McKinley's death, Theodore Roosevelt, not quite forty-three years old, became the youngest man to serve as president of the United States, a record he still holds. The Roosevelt family that moved into the White House in 1901 consisted of Theodore's second wife, Edith Kermit Carow Roosevelt, and their five children, ranging in age from four to fourteen, and his teenage daughter from his

PLATE 12

The new Executive Office Building had ample room for staff and press. This 1908 photograph of the clerks' office by Harris & Ewing shows an open workroom such as had always been known at the White House. The president and cabinet had adjoining rooms connected by double doors, but the main office was that of the president's secretary, who presided over the staff and stood between the president and the press.

first marriage. It had been several years since so many children had lived in the Executive Mansion, and the eight-room family quarters were very cramped. What had been a rather sedate White House became now very active. Ike Hoover, a White House usher who would from 1913 to 1933 serve as chief usher, commented in his memoir, "A nervous person had no business around the White House in those days. He was sure to be a wreck in a very short time."[5]

In 1902, Frances Benjamin Johnston requested and received permission to photograph the Roosevelt family at the White House, her fourth administration. Although most of her compositions are posed, several are more candid. She not only made visual records of the children with their various pets but, great recorder that she was, also gave glimpses into their personalities.

The cramped family quarters and overcrowded office area would be addressed in 1902 during a major White House renovation overseen by the architect Charles McKim. Photographs taken of this project outline the extensive work done during the renovation and the finished result. Many of these images were compiled in an album presented to the Roosevelts by McKim.[6]

Choosing not to run for a second elective term, Theodore Roosevelt and his family left the White House on March 4, 1909. Prior to leaving office, he was heard to remark, "Perhaps others have lived longer in this place and enjoyed it quite as much; but none have ever really had more fun out of it than we have."[7]

NOTES

1. Robert A. Mayer, "Photographing the American Presidency," *Image* 27, no. 3 (September 1984): 19. A stereograph is a card with two nearly identical images. When it is examined with a special viewer called a stereoscope, a three-dimensional effect is achieved.

2. William Seale, *The President's House* (Washington, D.C.: White House Historical Association, 1986), 630.

3. Robert H. Ferrell, "The Expanding White House," in *The White House: The First Two Hundred Years,* ed. Frank Freidel and William Pencak (Boston: Northeastern University Press, 1994), 104.

4. Frances Benjamin Johnston, also in attendance to photograph the exposition, is credited with having captured the last photograph of McKinley alive.

5. Irwin Hood Hoover, *Forty-Two Years in the White House* (Boston: Houghton Mifflin, 1934), 28.

6. The album is part of the collection of Sagamore Hill National Historic Site, the Roosevelt family home in Oyster Bay, New York. Another set of these photographs is in the collection of the Avery Architecture Library, Columbia University.

7. Quoted in Hoover, *Forty-Two Years,* 30.

The Green Room as completed in 1902.

Theodore Roosevelt's White House

JOHN ALLEN GABLE

THEODORE ROOSEVELT remade the presidency and reinvented the White House, and his models for both have lasted a century. He brought the president to center stage in the drama of American democracy. He made the president an activist world leader. He made the president a domestic "steward of the people" who regulated big business, protected the consumer, and preserved 230 million acres of parks, forest and wildlife preserves, and National Monuments for the "unborn generations." He saw the White House as a "bully pulpit" for preaching the doctrines of the "strenuous life," "the big stick," and the "Square Deal." In short, Theodore Roosevelt established what has been called the "modern presidency."[1] The changes he wrought in the presidency were profound and lasting, as Walter Lippmann wrote in 1935:

> He became for me the image of a great leader and the prototype of Presidents. The impression is indelible and, if I wished, I could not even now erase it. So persistent is it that in any complete confession I think I should have to say that I have been less than just to his successors because they were not like him. . . . The historians will say, I am convinced, that Theodore Roosevelt began the work of turning the American mind in the direction which it had to go in the Twentieth Century.[2]

Roosevelt's reinvention of the White House was part of his transformation of the presidency and is reflected in the fact that it was TR who officially changed the name of the president's residence from the Executive Mansion to the White House.[3] But when Theodore Roosevelt came to the presidency in 1901, because an assassin's bullet had felled William McKinley, the future of the White House was much in doubt.

The Executive Mansion was sadly in need of serious repair; the interior had become a Victorian hodgepodge; and there was a severe shortage of space, accom-

Theodore Roosevelt with his sons, Archie and Quentin. Photograph by Frances Benjamin Johnston, ca. 1904.

panied by a deficiency in design for living, entertaining, and working in the old house. In 1901 two very different but equally drastic alternatives were offered for the future of the White House. First Lady Caroline Harrison and later Colonel Theodore A. Bingham of the Army Corps of Engineers, who was head of public buildings in Washington, had presented proposals for above-ground additions that would have greatly expanded the White House into a sprawling complex, a reflection of the Louvre and other palaces in Europe. Colonel Bingham's design included two new wings, each a rotunda topped by a dome.[4] The other alternative was to preserve the White House as a historic monument or to use it as an office building and build a new executive domicile elsewhere in the capital city. The Washington philanthropist Mary Foote Henderson at her own cost ordered designs made for a new presidential residence to stand on Meridian Hill. Daniel H. Burnham, the great Chicago architect who in 1901 was appointed as one of four government commissioners to consider the future of Washington's public lands and buildings, proposed that a new presidential house be built on the site of the Naval Observatory, where today the vice president occupies the old admiral's residence. Burnham would have used the White House as executive offices.[5]

Less than a year after coming into office, Theodore Roosevelt rejected both the Harrison-Bingham and Henderson-Burnham alternatives. TR said to Charles Moore of the Commission on Public Lands and Buildings, "You tell the newspapermen that Mrs. Roosevelt and I are firmly of the opinion that the President should live nowhere else than in the White House." Mr. and Mrs. Roosevelt then turned to Charles F. McKim of McKim, Mead & White, arguably the most famous architectural firm in the history of monumental American building, to plan and carry out the repair, renovation, expansion, and decoration of the White House in 1902.[6]

Charles F. McKim's renovation of the White House introduced steel beams and concrete into the structure. The soot- and grease-stained basement of the house was rebuilt to become a needed entrance area and hallway, its historic groin vaulting plastered in snowy white. The East Room was dramatically changed from a cluttered Victorian parlor into a bright, open, and imposing French-style ballroom. The State Dining Room was enlarged by one-third, absorbing the area of the old Grand Staircase. The old dining room could seat fifty to sixty people; the remodeled dining room could seat more than one hundred. The decor of the State Dining Room was handsome and distinctively Georgian, with its highly waxed, mellow, dark brown oak paneling. Decades later the rich oak paneling was painted over, first in green and now in white, a redecoration that obscures the McKim-

Edith Roosevelt, 1902, in a photographic study for a portrait by Théobald Chartran.

Roosevelt legacy and is unfortunate from an aesthetic standpoint. A new Grand Staircase, perfect for Roosevelt's impressive presidential entrances, was installed connecting the living quarters with the staterooms.[7]

Edith Kermit Roosevelt, the first lady, had complained that domestic life in the White House was "like living over the store." But in the renovation the second-floor offices were transformed into bedrooms and family quarters. A new West Wing was added as an executive office complex. Low in height, classical in design, unobtrusive, the new West Wing in no way detracted visually from the original White House.[8]

The interior decoration of the White House, under the supervision of Charles McKim and the watchful eye of Edith Roosevelt, was carried out largely by the noted New York firms of Herter Brothers and Leon Marcotte & Company and by A. H. Davenport & Company of Boston. In the 1860s Marcotte had likely handled the redecoration of the Roosevelt brownstone at 28 East 20th Street, Manhattan, TR's birthplace.[9]

The new White House interior was given a distinctive American character by the game heads and skins the president ordered strategically placed about the mansion. The State Dining Room was given a baronial look by mounted elk, bison, deer, moose, and other heads—eleven in all—and there were bearskin rugs in the Green Room and the Blue Room.[10]

The carved mantel in the new State Dining Room at first featured lions, but in 1908, not long before he left the White House, TR had these replaced by American bison.[11] Roosevelt thought that buffalo had great artistic potential. He also wanted to substitute bison for the famous lions in front of the New York Public Library. He wrote to the Fifteenth Annual Convention of the American Institute of Architects:

> The lion, because of the way in which his mane lends itself to use in stone, has always been a favorite for decorative purposes in architecture. He has in architecture become universally acclimatized and there is no objection to his use anywhere. But we happen to have here on this continent, in the bison with its shaggy frontlet and mane and short curved horns, a beast which equally lends itself to decorative use and which possesses the advantage of being our own. I earnestly wish that the conventions of architecture here in America would be shaped as to include widespread use of the bison's head; and in a case like that of the New York Public Library there would be advantage from every standpoint in substituting two complete bisons' figures for the preposterous lions, apparently in the preliminary stages of epilepsy, which now front on and disgrace Fifth Avenue.[12]

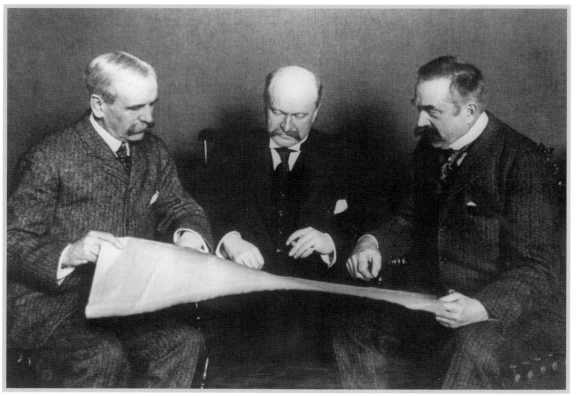

Charles McKim, William R. Mead, and Stanford White, architects for the Roosevelt renovations of 1902. Charles McKim was the principal. The involvement of the other two partners was minimal.

The original stone mantel with the bison, removed during the Truman renovation, is now stored in the Harry S. Truman Library in Independence, Missouri.[13] But First Lady Jacqueline Kennedy replicated the mantel, and the bison are once again in the State Dining Room.

We should not let our postmodern sensibilities be distracted by the heads and skins and carved bison. The interior of the White House in the 1902 renovation was elegantly neoclassical in character and in many essentials is the White House interior we know today. The renovation was accomplished in about six months at a cost of $467,105.60. We know that McKim worked in too much haste and with more attention to outward appearance than to structural needs, necessitating the massive rebuilding and renovation that took place in 1949–52, during the administration of Harry S. Truman. But in spite of all the changes, reconstruction, and renovations that have taken place since 1902, the interior of the White House and the West Wing remains to a considerable extent the product of Charles F. McKim's design and vision.[14]

McKim used the terms "restore" and "restoration" to describe what he had done, and Theodore Roosevelt also habitually used these words in talking about what happened in 1902. He said in his Annual Message: "Through a wise provision of the Congress at its last session the White House, which had become disfigured by incongruous additions and changes, has now been restored to what it was planned to be by Washington." But as William Seale and others have noted, while the exterior of the White House looked much the same, with the exception of the West Wing addition, the interior of the Executive Mansion was vastly changed, both from what it had been in 1901 and from what it had been designed to be by James Hoban.[15]

The chaste federal-style interior of Hoban had been replaced, in Seale's words, by a "more elaborate Georgian style." The words "restore" and "restoration" are therefore misnomers. This was, in short, almost a new house. It was a Beaux Arts amplification of eighteenth-century American design. The State Dining Room resembled a hall in an eighteenth-century English estate rather than rooms of the period in the United States. Seale writes: "McKim's new image of the White House was sophisticated and upper class in tone, where the traditional aspect had been bourgeois; it was cosmopolitan." At that time and since, the renovated or reinvented White House was described as "imperial" in appearance. "Roosevelt's White House shouted magnificence," says Seale.[16]

There is no denying the truth of what Seale and others have said about the radical nature of the changes that took place in the interior design and decor of the White House. But further and differing perspectives are possible on the McKim-Roosevelt White House. In other words, there is more than one valid way to describe what happened in 1902.

Theodore Roosevelt wrote to an old friend on December 8, 1902: "The changes in the White House have transformed it from a shabby likeness to the ground floor of the Astor House [Hotel] into a simple and dignified dwelling for the head of a great republic. I am very much pleased with it."[17] On another occasion he described the McKim White House as having a "simple and stately dignity." "Only a yahoo could have his taste offended, and excepting a yahoo, only a very base partisan politician would complain of it," Roosevelt wrote Lawrence F. Abbott of *Outlook* magazine.[18] Ellen Maury Slayden, the wife of a congressman from Texas, wrote, "If Roosevelt had never done anything else, the metamorphosis

The East Room as completed in 1902.

PLATE 12. *Alice Roosevelt, the president's daughter, in a signature portrait, photographed in the East Room by Frances Benjamin Johnston, 1906, hand colored. She moved to the White House as a teenager, and as she grew into a young woman she made it her daily business to shock and amuse the public with outrageous acts designed to seem out of character for one so highly placed. The performance was to continue for her entire long life.*

PLATE 13. Theodore Roosevelt, *by John Singer Sargent, 1903. The president, age forty-three, poses for an instant with characteristic force and determination at the foot of the Grand Staircase.*

PLATE 14. *Family Dining Room today, with Edith Roosevelt's portrait by Théobald Chartran. Among colonial revival furnishings of the sort she loved, Mrs. Roosevelt seems at home in this room more than any other at the White House. Her flawless judgment in matters of form was a powerful influence on Theodore Roosevelt. Many customs at the White House today, such as the after-dinner musicales, began with her.*

PLATE 15. Eleanor Roosevelt, *by Douglas Chandor, 1949. The White House became Eleanor Roosevelt's spring-board for humanitarian causes that took her far beyond the traditional duties of first lady. Although for some twenty years her predecessors had been solicited for such endeavors, Eleanor Roosevelt actively sought them. She and FDR lived at the White House for thirteen years, longer than any other presidential couple. This portrait shows her in busy retirement at her Hudson River estate, probably at that time the most highly respected and controversial woman in the world.*

PLATE 16. *The Blue Room as redecorated for President Truman in 1952. Theodore Roosevelt's reproduction furniture of fifty years earlier was refurbished. A rich royal blue, relieved by white and gold, made the elegant color scheme.*

PLATE 18. *President Lyndon B. Johnson addresses the nation from the Oval Office. During the 1960s the Oval Office became a familiar television background for presidential addresses, used by LBJ more than any other location.*

PLATE 17. *The Blue Room as redecorated during the John F. Kennedy administration eleven years after Truman's Blue Room. The last of the interiors redecorated under Jacqueline Kennedy's "restoration," the historic oval room provided a dramatic background for a vigorous presidency and established a historical tone of decor for the state rooms that prevails today.*

PLATE 19. *The Nixon family at dinner in the second-floor President's Dining Room. David and Julie Nixon Eisenhower join her parents and her sister, Tricia, at a rather typical "at home" dinner. Although a small kitchen is nearby, many meals served here are prepared two floors below and brought up on a mechanical dumbwaiter.*

PLATE 20.

President Gerald Ford with his family in the Oval Office on his inauguration day, August 9, 1974. The only man to hold the office of president who had not stood in a national election for it or for the vice presidency, Gerald R. Ford was a highly respected member of Congress whom President Richard Nixon had appointed to the vice presidency. As circumstances unfolded, he soon ascended to the presidency, which was vacated on President Nixon's resignation. The nation's two hundredth anniversary fell during Ford's administration.

GERALD R. FORD LIBRARY

JIMMY CARTER LIBRARY

PLATE 21. *President Carter delivering an address from the Oval Office, 1979. Like FDR in his fireside chats more than thirty years before, Carter made frequent use of the White House to help personalize as well as endorse his addresses to the American people.*

PLATE 22.
President and Mrs. Ronald Reagan face news photographers on the North Portico. The walls of newsmen are a feature of presidential life outside the stone walls. Here the Reagans greet the "wall" while awaiting guests for a state dinner.

PLATE 23. *President and Mrs. George Bush at a media picnic on the South Lawn. Picnics under tents on the South Lawn were a part of late-twentieth-century White House hospitality. Guests sometimes numbered in the thousands. Begun with President Lyndon B. Johnson's barbecues, they have continued with varying themes and ever-larger crowds.*

PLATE 24.
President and Mrs. Bill Clinton share a whisper at the state dinner for the two hundredth anniversary of John Adams's move to the White House, November 1, 1800.

PLATE 25. *A modern view of the White House from the north. George Washington personally staked the location of the White House in 1792. Every president since him has lived there, from John Adams to George W. Bush. All leave their marks, but the timeless image remains unchanged, today one of the most familiar symbols in the world.*

Jules Guerin's dreamy 1903 image in pencil on canvas of the south side of the White House as remodeled by Theodore Roosevelt in 1902.

He devotes a few moments to San Domingo

He hands Mr. Castro a few

He jumps on the U. S. Senate

He dashes off an essay about the race question

He lands on the Standard Oil Co.

He attends a banquet in New York

He superintends the preparations for Inauguration Day

He passes a hot message to the Senate

He pauses for a moment to make plans for a hunting trip

"One of Theodore Roosevelt's quiet days."

of the White House from a gilded barn to a comfortable residence . . . would entitle him to his country's gratitude."[19] Glenn Brown, a well-known architect and the secretary of the American Institute of Architects, said in 1906 that the White House, which over the years had become "an architectural aberration," was now "a charming and refined mansion."[20]

PLATE 13

Yes, McKim's White House was a palace; structurally it was a reinvention of the Executive Mansion and not a restoration. But the McKim-Roosevelt White House was also "refined," "charming," "dignified," and "stately," as was said. And, yes, it was even "simple," particularly in comparison to contemporary mansions in Newport or on Fifth Avenue, in contrast to most European palaces, and when we consider the hodgepodge interior of the White House that was replaced.

Could the renovation have been different and better? In structural terms, the answer is a definite yes. But as to form and decor, the alternatives at the time had been to expand the White House beyond recognition or to abandon it. Under these options, the interior of the house probably would have been changed as drastically as the exterior—adapted to use as an office building, or frozen in time as a museum. Moreover, the McKim interior surely suited the mansion, whatever else may be said. The McKim-Roosevelt White House has now stood the proverbial test of time; it has proven to be highly adaptable; and after a hundred years it is hallowed by historical associations. It is, in short, a success.

The reinvention of the White House was part of Theodore Roosevelt's remaking of the presidency. How was this the case? First, the presidency was institutionalized as never before, as seen in the building of the new West Wing. Second, for the first time the president was a world leader, and because Roosevelt worked in a world of monarchs and empires, the White House became a palace—a palace in appearance, appointments, and functions. For the first time, the White House was regularly described as a "court" and a "salon." There was a steady flow of foreign visitors, such as Prince Henry of Prussia, Baron Paul Estournelles de Constant of France, John Morley and H. G. Wells from England, the Italian historian Guglielmo Ferrarro, Prince Tsai Fu of China, and Prince Louis of Battenberg, in addition to the perpetual presence of foreign ambassadors who were friends and confidants of the president, including J. J. Jusserand of France, Baron Speck von Sternberg of Germany, and Lord Bryce of Great Britain.[21]

Third, Roosevelt was a president with a broad-ranging agenda of reform. He believed that a president should have programs to meet the nation's needs. His agenda was evident in the meetings at the White House of the first national governors' conference in 1908, the Joint Conservation Congress in 1909, and the

White House conference on children in 1909, as well as in the visits to the White House of people such as Jacob Riis, Susan B. Anthony, Lincoln Steffens, and John Mitchell of the United Mine Workers.[22]

Fourth, Roosevelt saw the presidency as properly concerned and involved with anything that was of importance or interest to the American people. This emphasis was reflected in the White House meeting on October 9, 1905, that led to the founding of the National Collegiate Athletic Association, and the White House visits of such diverse figures and celebrities as Billy Sunday and Cardinal Gibbons, Buffalo Bill and John L. Sullivan, Robert E. Peary and Joel Chandler Harris and the naturalist John Burroughs. The ultimate open house took place on January 1, 1907, at the traditional New Year's Day public reception, when Roosevelt shook hands with more than eight thousand people, winning a place for himself in the *Guinness Book of World Records.*[23]

Fifth, whether or not TR's presidency can accurately be called imperial, a traditional function of monarchs had been patronage of the arts and letters; and it is certainly true that Roosevelt believed the president should take a leadership role in promoting culture and the arts and letters. In his *Autobiography* (1913) Roosevelt discusses this cultural leadership in his chapter on conservation. He explains that many of his conservation measures are for the economic benefit of the people. Then he says, "In addition certain things were done of which the economic bearing was more remote, but which bore directly on our welfare, because they add to the beauty of living and therefore to the joy of life." He next discusses, in a chapter on irrigation projects and national forests, his promotion of an artistic coinage designed by Augustus Saint-Gaudens and the idea of a commission governing fine arts, "an unpaid body of the best architects, painters, and sculptors in the country, to advise the Government as to the erection and decoration of all new buildings."[24]

Roosevelt's cultural leadership was also seen in the establishment of the Freer Gallery in Washington, his renovation of the White House, and his support of a master plan for the capital city based upon Pierre L'Enfant's original plan for Washington. There was also an endless procession to White House dinners of luminaries from the world of arts and letters, such as the writers Henry James, Hamlin Garland, Edith Wharton, and his friend Owen Wister; the historian Henry Adams; the stained-glass artist John La Farge, the illustrator Howard Pyle, and the noted battle-scene painter Frank Millet; the sculptor Augustus Saint-Gaudens; and many others. To Edwin Arlington Robinson, Roosevelt gave a government sinecure to provide a living while he wrote poetry. The White House patronage of the arts was further carried out through actual performances in the East Room.[25]

Edith Kermit Carow Roosevelt as first lady was a very important power in the

Roosevelt administration. More than her husband, she was responsible for the renovation of the White House. She also established the White House collection of portraits of first ladies and expanded the collection of presidential china begun by First Lady Caroline Harrison, both displayed in the new lower entrance hallway. Mrs. Roosevelt's secretary, Isabella Hagner, was one of the first women to assume an executive role in the White House. She was "head aide, general manager, and superintendent," said Major Archie Butt, the president's military aide. Mrs. Roosevelt's White House concerts or "musicales," as she called them, deserve attention in any history of the Executive Mansion.[26]

While musical events had been held before in the White House, Edith Roosevelt began the tradition of important and regular concerts on a grand scale. The first lady held an average of about eight musicales a year, with approximately 350 attending the events in the East Room, usually fairly late in the evening, sometimes in the afternoon. According to the music historian Elise K. Kirk, Mrs. Roosevelt held the first full concerts by noted pianists, the first full performance of an opera, and the first clavichord performance in the White House.[27]

Mrs. Roosevelt also acquired a fine concert grand piano for the White House, a gift in 1903 from Steinway & Sons. The magnificent case was covered with gold leaf and decorated with the coats of arms of the thirteen original states. Inside the lid was a handsome painting by Thomas Wilmer Dewing portraying the nine muses paying court to a woman representing the American republic. The handsome piano, now at the Smithsonian Institution, served the White House until 1938.[28]

Such great pianists as Poland's composer-statesman Ignace Paderewski, the handsome Italian Ferruccio Busoni, the spirited Olga Saaroff, the respected Fannie Bloomfield Zeisler, and the fabled Josef Hofmann played in the East Room. Other musicales featured the legendary cellist Pablo Casals, the beloved contralto Madame Schumann-Heink, the Philadelphia Symphony Orchestra, and the Vienna Male Voice Choir. Mrs. Roosevelt insisted on featuring American as well as European music and artists at the White House. Arthur Nevin's so-called American Indian opera, *Poia,* was presented in concert in 1907; the Marine Band played Scott Joplin's *Maple Leaf Rag,* which was Alice Roosevelt's idea; and, writes Kirk, "Probably more Edward MacDowell was played in the White House during the Roosevelt administration than anywhere in America at this time." The tradition of major concerts in the White House was continued by the Taft and Wilson administrations and became an important part of American cultural life.[29] Theodore Roosevelt, whose interest in music was confined to marches and hymns, had little to do with the concerts except to attend them and afterward to present the guest artists with autographed copies of his book *The Rough Riders* or signed photographs of himself in silver frames.[30]

PLATE 14

If Eleanor Roosevelt, Edith and Theodore's niece, is the model for the modern, activist first lady, then Edith Kermit Roosevelt as much or more than anyone else is the epitome of the successful traditional first lady. TR wrote in a letter in 1902: "I do not think my eyes are blinded by affection when I say that she has combined to a degree I have never seen in any other woman the power of being the best of wives and mothers, the wisest manager of the household, and at the same time the ideal great lady and mistress of the White House." Major Butt said that Edith Roosevelt never made a mistake during her years as first lady.[31]

No discussion of the Roosevelt White House would be complete, or near complete, without mention of the Roosevelt children: Alice (born to his first wife in 1884), Theodore Junior (born 1887), Kermit (born 1889), Ethel (born 1891), Archibald (born 1894), and Quentin (born 1897). "Princess Alice" was one of the nation's first modern celebrities and for eighty years was famous simply for being famous. In time she was known as "Washington's other monument." The four boys, Ted, Kermit, Archie, and Quentin, were much-decorated war heroes. Quentin was killed in World War I. Kermit and Ted were in both world wars and died in the service during World War II. Archie earned the distinction of being the only American with a total disability status from two world wars. Ethel kept the home fires burning in Oyster Bay, New York; preserved the Roosevelt home, Sagamore Hill, for future generations; and lived to visit Jimmy Carter in the White House. For a hundred years stories of the Roosevelt children—their pet snakes, adventures, and antics in the White House—have filled newspapers and books. Chief Usher Ike Hoover recalled, "A nervous person had no business around the White House."[32] Their adventures were chronicled for later generations in two beloved classics, *Theodore Roosevelt's Letters to His Children* (1919) and *The White House Gang* (1929) by Earle Looker, a "member of the gang."[33]

Aside from the fun, something important happened when the Sagamore Hill tribe invaded the White House. It was not the first time children or presidential progeny lived in the White House, though perhaps never before in such numbers. But now the concept and reality of a "first family" took on new and significant meaning. Ike Hoover wrote many years after the Roosevelts left the White House:

Probably no administration has taken such a curious hold upon the people as that of Theodore Roosevelt. It made no difference where you turned, it was the same. Every little event concerning any of the family . . . was broadcast through the news-

President Theodore Roosevelt and the third-term nomination.

papers. No family have ever been written up so much; and the strange part of it was that while the newspapers exaggerated the stories about other Presidential families, in the case of the Roosevelts they had to tone down the facts for fear of being disbelieved! News was always abundant, and it was a poor reporter indeed who did not pick up a column or two any day during these strenuous times.[34]

"Princess Alice" Roosevelt had a color named after her, "Alice Blue," and countless popular songs were dedicated to her. Her visit to the Far East was like a royal tour, and her celebrity status on this trip was an asset to American diplomacy. Alice's White House debut and wedding were among the most famous social events of the twentieth century. The other Roosevelt children had streets and towns named after them—there is a Kermit, West Virginia, and an Ethel, West Virginia—and prints and photographs of the family were hung on walls everywhere.[35]

The Roosevelts spent their summers at Sagamore Hill in Oyster Bay, Long Island, a home that was soon called the "summer White House." Improvements in communication and transportation now made it possible for the president to carry on the business of government at a great distance from Washington. Much of the negotiations with the Russians and Japanese that led to the Portsmouth Treaty in 1905, ending the Russo-Japanese War and winning the Nobel Peace Prize for the president, were carried on at Oyster Bay. And it was from Oyster Bay that the first transglobal message was sent and returned in 1903 after the completion of the Pacific cable.[36]

The Roosevelts had a second presidential retreat, Pine Knot, in Albemarle County, Virginia, near Charlottesville. Purchased by Edith Roosevelt for $280 in 1905, Pine Knot was used on eight occasions at various times of the year by the president and first lady and members of their family.[37] Pine Knot was the first of the many rustic presidential retreats that culminated in Franklin D. Roosevelt's Shangri-La, today's Camp David.

Both Sagamore Hill and Pine Knot showed the essential simplicity of Theodore and Edith Roosevelt's lifestyle. Sagamore Hill, a rambling twenty-two-room Queen Anne revival wooden country house, was comfortable, but no one ever thought of the famous Roosevelt residence as palatial or fashionable. Pine Knot was a simple wood-frame Virginia mountain cottage, without plumbing or electricity, originally built as a sharecropper's house. A newspaper man wrote that Pine Knot was "probably quite the most unpretentious habitation ever owned by a president of the United States."[38]

Even today the magic and the appeal of Theodore Roosevelt's family lingers on. Stephen E. Ambrose wrote in 1998, "The Roosevelts—not just TR but the whole family—are larger than life, real heroes, the kind of men and women we would all like to be."[39] TR's own magic was particularly evident at table, at the luncheons and dinners in the White House, when the president assembled guests who reflected his myriad and eclectic interests and his broad-ranging agenda for the nation. Rough Riders, scientists, social workers, politicians, and writers would be juxtaposed about the table. Owen Wister recalled, "To see him conduct a lunch with Bat Masterson from the alkali, and a clergyman from Vermont, and a philanthropist from the Philippines, and a bi-metalist from Aberdeen, and a leading lady in Newport society, and Lord Bryce, and everybody's wife or husband, if they had one, all seated around the table, and each brought into the talk for his particular contribution, was something never to forget."[40]

Historians have pointed to one particular luncheon as showing the intellectual brilliance of the White House during Roosevelt's tenure. On January 12, 1905, Theodore and Edith Roosevelt entertained at lunch Henry Adams, John La Farge, Augustus Saint-Gaudens, and Henry James.[41] But without question the most famous meal in the Roosevelt White House was on October 16, 1901, when Booker T. Washington, the educator and African American political leader, dined with the president and his family. This was a first for the White House, and a last for the Roosevelt administration, which was savagely attacked by the white press of the South. A Tennessee newspaper said the Booker T. Washington dinner was "the most damnable outrage ever."[42]

Theodore Roosevelt's remade presidency and reinvented White House were often described, then and later, as "imperial." As we have seen, there is an aptness to this description as applied to the elegant renovated McKim-Roosevelt White

House; and there is a literal truth in the term, since by then the United States had acquired an overseas empire, including Puerto Rico, Hawaii, the Philippines, and other assorted islands. But make no mistake about it: Theodore Roosevelt rejected the adjective "imperial" to describe either the White House or his administration and was not in the least pleased to see the term "imperial" applied to his Square Deal and Big Stick policies.[43]

To Roosevelt, the American overseas empire was a product of circumstances and would probably not be permanent. He saw American world power as on the side of peace and progress. For him, a powerful chief executive was not a threat to democracy at home but the most effective instrumentality available to serve the modern needs of the American people. He wrote to a friend in 1905, "The more I see of the Czar, the Kaiser, and the Mikado, the better I am content with democracy, even if we have to include the American newspaper as one of its assets."[44]

The charges of presidential usurpation of power and the cartoons showing Roosevelt as Julius Caesar or Napoleon bothered the president greatly. Didn't everyone realize that he was more like George Washington than some foreign monarch? To the historian Sir George Otto Trevelyan, Roosevelt wrote in 1908: "I don't think that any harm comes from the concentration of power in one man's hands, provided the holder does not keep it for more than a certain, definite time, and then returns to the people from whom he sprang."[45] And so it was that Theodore Roosevelt refused to run again in 1908, when a third term was his for the asking or taking. And he did want to run in 1908. "I have had a good run for my money," he wrote to his son Kermit, "and I should have liked to stay in as President if I had felt it was right for me to do so."[46] Refusing to run in 1908 was Roosevelt's great abnegation, and he thought it would definitively prove the purity of his soul and the integrity of the office he had remade into the "modern presidency." What he had done in 1908 was one of the problems he faced when deciding to run again in 1912. He knew that he would be accused—as he was—of Caesarism, selfish ambition, and going back on his word. But he ran again in 1912 because he believed there were higher considerations than the fate of his reputation. Running in 1912, it could be argued, was therefore a greater personal sacrifice than not running in 1908. It could also be argued, of course, that Roosevelt made the wrong decision in both 1908 and 1912. Certain it is that one decision led directly to the other.[47]

When Theodore Roosevelt left the White House in 1909, however, the dimensions of his legacy looked large and lasting, and today that is also the verdict of the public and many historians. The White House historian Esther Singleton wrote

Ted Roosevelt with his macaw, Eli Yale. Photograph by Frances Benjamin Johnston.

in 1907 that each president had "impressed his taste . . . upon the White House during his administration," only to have his changes "swept away by his successor." But Theodore Roosevelt's changes to the White House had been "so complete" that she wondered if perhaps Roosevelt's White House was here to stay.[48] William Seale writes: "Presidents through history had imposed their personal styles upon the White House. Now the White House would begin to impose a presidential style upon them."[49] Much the same could be said of TR's "modern presidency." Future presidents would have to live up to it in what Henry R. Luce called "the American Century." In describing her father's administration, Ethel Roosevelt Derby once said to me, "It was a brave, bright morning."[50] And so it was.

NOTES

1. The best accounts of Theodore Roosevelt's administration are Lewis L. Gould, *The Presidency of Theodore Roosevelt* (Lawrence: University Press of Kansas, 1991); William H. Harbaugh, *The Life and Times of Theodore Roosevelt* (1961), rev. ed. (New York: Oxford University Press, 1975), chaps. 9–22; Edmund Morris, *Theodore Rex* (New York: Random House, 2001); George E. Mowry, *The Era of Theodore Roosevelt and the Birth of Modern America, 1900–1912* (New York: Harper & Row, 1958). On TR as the first modern president, see Richard M. Pious, *The Presidency* (Boston: Allyn and Bacon, 1996), 48–49, 57–58; Clinton Rossiter, *The American Presidency* (1956), rev. ed. (Baltimore: Johns Hopkins University Press, 1987), 87–90. On the president as "steward of the people," see Roosevelt's *An Autobiography,* in Hermann Hagedorn, ed., *The National Edition of the Works of Theodore Roosevelt* (New York: Charles Scribner's Sons, 1926), 20:347–48; for the "unborn generations," see Roosevelt's *Literary Essays,* ibid., 12:425. On the White House or presidency as a "bully pulpit," see Lyman Abbott, "A Review of President Roosevelt's Administration, Part 4, Its Influence on Patriotism and Public Service," *Outlook* 91 (February 27, 1909): 430; Gould, *Presidency of Theodore Roosevelt,* 10; George Haven Putnam, introduction to 1926 reprint of *The Winning of the West,* in *National Edition,* 9:x. On the "strenuous life," see Roosevelt's *The Strenuous Life* (1899) in *National Edition,* 13:319–31; on the "big stick," see Roosevelt's speech to the Minnesota State Fair, September 2, 1901, ibid., 474, and *Autobiography* (1913), ibid., 20:524. On the "Square Deal," see three of Roosevelt's speeches in 1903, in Theodore Roosevelt, *Presidential Addresses and State Papers: European Addresses,* Homeward Bound ed. (New York: Review of Reviews, 1910), 1:371, 2:446, 481.

2. Walter Lippmann, "A Tribute to Theodore Roosevelt" (1935), reprinted in *Theodore Roosevelt Association Journal* 24, no. 1 (2000): 4–5.

3. William Seale, *The President's House,* 2 vols. (Washington, D.C.: White House Historical Association, 1986), 654.

4. Ibid., 535–37, 586–90, 637–38, 640–45, 653–57; *The White House: An Historic Guide,* 15th ed. (Washington, D.C.: White House Historical Association, 1982), 133–44. Presidents Chester A. Arthur and Grover Cleveland had also considered greatly enlarging the White House.

5. Seale, *President's House,* 639–40, 654–57.

6. Ibid., 656–64, quotation on 656–57.

7. On the 1902 renovation of the White House, see Betty C. Monkman, *The White House: Its Historic Furnishings and First Families* (Washington, D.C.: White House Historical Association, 2000), 185–97; Sylvia Jukes Morris, *Edith Kermit Roosevelt: Portrait of a First Lady* (New York: Coward, McCann & Geoghegan, 1980), 221–23, 237–58; Seale, *President's House,* 657–84; Esther Singleton, *The Story of the White House,* 2 vols. (New York: McClure, 1907), 2:253–307. On the State Dining Room, also see Marian Burros, "Ruffles and Flourishes to Hail the New Chief," *New York Times,* November 2, 2000; *White House: Historic Guide,* 58–61.

8. Quoted in Morris, *Edith Kermit Roosevelt,* 222. On the West Wing, see Singleton, *Story of the White House,* 2:284–87; *White House: Historic Guide,* pp. 92–101. The West Wing was doubled in size in 1909 and has subsequently been further enlarged. The famous Oval Office was added by William Howard Taft and moved by FDR to the southeast corner in 1934. A meeting room near the Oval Office was named the Roosevelt Room by Richard M. Nixon and is decorated with paintings and bronzes of Theodore and Franklin D. Roosevelt.

9. Monkman, *White House,* 185–97; Seale, *President's House,* 676–78; David M. Kahn, "The Theodore Roosevelt Birthplace in New York City," *Antiques* 117, no. 1 (July 1979): 176–81. Other firms involved in the interior decoration were Edward F. Caldwell & Company of New York and W. B. Moses & Sons of Washington as well as two other Washington firms.

10. Burros, "Ruffles and Flourishes to Hail the New Chief"; Singleton, *Story of the White House,* vol. 2, photographs facing 256, 293, 304; *White House: Historic Guide,* 58–61.

11. Theodore Roosevelt to William Mitchell Kendall, December 18, 1908, *The Letters of Theodore Roosevelt,* ed. Elting E. Morison, John M. Blum, and Alfred D. Chandler Jr., 8 vols. (Cambridge, Mass.: Harvard University Press, 1951–54), 6:1430.

12. Theodore Roosevelt, letter, in *Theodore Roosevelt Cyclopedia* (1941), ed. Albert Bushnell Hart and Herbert Ronald Ferleger, 2d rev. ed. John Allen Gable (Oyster Bay, N.Y.: Theodore Roosevelt Association and Meckler Corp., 1989), 25.

13. The mantelpiece remains in the collection of the Truman Library.

14. Seale, *President's House,* 678, 1024–51. Monkman (*White House,* 186) writes: "Interior decoration in the White House continued to change in the new century, but the architectural spaces of today's house remain essentially those created in 1902."

15. Theodore Roosevelt, Annual Message to Congress, 1902, in *National Edition,* 15:167–68; Seale, *President's House,* 661–62, 683–84.

16. Seale, *President's House,* 682, 717.

17. Theodore Roosevelt to Maria Longworth Storer, December 8, 1902, in *Letters,* ed. Morison, Blum, and Chandler, 3:391–92.

18. Theodore Roosevelt to Lawrence F. Abbott, March 14, 1904, ibid., 4:751–52. Also see Theodore Roosevelt to Nicholas Murray Butler, June 3, 1904, ibid., 814–19.

19. Quoted in Morris, *Edith Kermit Roosevelt,* 241.

20. Quoted ibid., 257.

21. Roosevelt's appointments and guests are listed in chronologies at the end of volumes 2, 4, 6, and 8 of *Letters,* ed. Morison, Blum, and Chandler. On John Morley's visit to the White House, see Joseph Bucklin Bishop, *Theodore Roosevelt and His Time* (New York: Charles Scribner's Sons,

1920), 1:337–42. On TR's White House as a "salon" and "court," see Nelson M. Blake, "Ambassadors at the Court of Theodore Roosevelt," *Mississippi Valley Historical Review* 24 (1955): 179–206; Richard H. Collin, *Theodore Roosevelt, Culture, Diplomacy, and Expansion: A New View of American Imperialism* (Baton Rouge: Louisiana State University Press, 1985), chaps. 1–3.

22. On the first governors' conference and the Joint Conservation Congress, see Harbaugh, *Theodore Roosevelt,* 317–19; also Roosevelt, *An Autobiography,* in *National Edition,* ed. Hagedorn, 20:400–402.

23. On the founding of the National Collegiate Athletic Association, see Theodore Roosevelt to George Gray, October 6, 1905, in *Letters,* ed. Morison, Blum, and Chandler, 5:46. On New Year's Day, 1907, see Edmund Morris, *The Rise of Theodore Roosevelt* (New York: Coward, McCann & Geoghegan, 1979), 27, 758.

24. Roosevelt, *An Autobiography,* in *National Edition,* ed. Hagedorn, 20:411. On artistic coinage, see Willard B. Gatewood, *Theodore Roosevelt and the Art of Controversy* (Baton Rouge: Louisiana State University Press, 1970), 213–35. The Commission of Fine Arts was appointed by President William Howard Taft in 1910 and still functions.

25. On the Freer Gallery, see Collin, *Culture, Diplomacy, and Expansion,* 6, 66–91. On the L'Enfant plan, see Seale, *President's House,* 654–59. On Edwin Arlington Robinson, see Theodore Roosevelt to Edward Arlington Robinson, March 27, 1905, in *Letters,* ed. Morison, Blum, and Chandler, 4:1145; Theodore Roosevelt to James H. Canfield, August 16, 1905, ibid., 4:1303. On Roosevelt and the arts and letters, see Edward Wagenknecht, *The Seven Worlds of Theodore Roosevelt* (New York: Longmans, Green, 1958), 31–84.

26. On Mrs. Roosevelt's contributions to the White House collections of portraits of first ladies and presidential china, see Monkman, *White House,* 192–97; Sylvia Morris, *Edith Kermit Roosevelt,* 254, 260; Seale, *President's House,* 680, 754, 909–10. On Isabella Hagner, see Archie Butt to his mother, June 30, 1908, in *Letters of Archie Butt,* ed. Lawrence F. Abbott (Garden City, N.Y.: Doubleday, Page, 1924), 54; Monkman, *White House,* 192; Sylvia Morris, *Edith Kermit Roosevelt,* 226.

27. Elise K. Kirk, *Music at the White House: A History of the American Spirit* (Urbana: University of Illinois Press, 1986), 169–71.

28. Ibid., 171–73.

29. On Mrs. Roosevelt's concerts, see ibid., 169–88, quotation on 171; Sylvia Morris, *Edith Kermit Roosevelt,* 235–37.

30. Kirk, *Music at the White House,* 190; Sylvia Morris, *Edith Kermit Roosevelt,* 235.

31. Theodore Roosevelt to Maria Longworth Storer, December 8, 1902, in *Letters,* ed. Morison, Blum, and Chandler, 3:391–92; Archie Butt to Clara Butt, November 18, 1908, in *Taft and Roosevelt: The Intimate Letters of Archie Butt, Military Aide,* 2 vols. (Garden City, N.Y.: Doubleday, Doran, 1930), 1:181.

32. Irwin Hood Hoover, *Forty-Two Years at the White House* (Boston: Houghton Mifflin, 1934), 28. Joan Patterson Kerr has biographical sketches of the Roosevelt children in her edition of TR's letters to his children, *A Bully Father: Theodore Roosevelt's Letters to His Children* (New York: Random House, 1995). Also see Edward J. Renehan Jr., *The Lion's Pride: Theodore Roosevelt and His Family in Peace and War* (New York: Oxford University Press, 1998). The best biography of Alice Roosevelt Longworth is Michael Teague, *Mrs. L: Conversations with Alice Roosevelt Longworth* (Garden City,

N.Y.: Doubleday, 1981). Also see Stacy Rozek Cordery, "'Princess Alice': The Life and Times of Alice Roosevelt Longworth," *Theodore Roosevelt Association Journal* 23, no. 4 (2000): 10–14. Mrs. Longworth's autobiography is Alice R. Longworth, *Crowded Hours* (New York: Charles Scribner's Sons, 1933). On Edith Roosevelt, Ethel Roosevelt Derby, and Alice R. Longworth, also see Betty Boyd Caroli, *The Roosevelt Women* (New York: Basic Books, 1998).

33. *Theodore Roosevelt's Letters to His Children* is vol. 19 in *National Edition;* Earle Looker, *The White House Gang* (New York: Fleming H. Revell, 1929).

34. Hoover, *Forty-Two Years at the White House,* 27.

35. Kermit is in Mingo County and Ethel is in Logan County, West Virginia. In Maplewood, New Jersey, there are streets named after Kermit and Quentin Roosevelt—Kermit Road and Quentin Court. Roosevelt Field on Long Island is named for Quentin Roosevelt, as is Roosevelt, Pennsylvania. On Alice Roosevelt Longworth's fame and diplomatic utility, see Stacy Rozek, "The First Daughter of the Land: Alice Roosevelt as Presidential Celebrity, 1902–1906," *Presidential Studies Quarterly* 19, no. 1 (Winter 1989): 51–70; Stacy Rozek Cordery, "Theodore Roosevelt's Private Diplomat: Alice Roosevelt and the 1905 Far East Junket," in *Theodore Roosevelt: Many-Sided American,* ed. Natalie A. Naylor, Douglas Brinkley, and John Allen Gable (Interlaken, N.Y.: Heart of the Lakes Publishing, 1992), 353–67.

36. The best chronicle of the Roosevelts' life at Sagamore Hill is Hermann Hagedorn, *The Roosevelt Family of Sagamore Hill* (New York: Macmillan, 1954). Also see Hermann Hagedorn and Gary G. Roth, *Sagamore Hill: An Historical Guide* (Oyster Bay, N.Y.: Theodore Roosevelt Association, 1977); Theodore Roosevelt Jr., *All in the Family* (New York: G. P. Putnam's Sons, 1929); Sherwin Gluck, *TR's Summer White House, Oyster Bay* (Oyster Bay, N.Y.: Sherwin Gluck, 1999).

37. William H. Harbaugh, *The Theodore Roosevelts' Retreat in Southern Albemarle: Pine Knot, 1905–1908* (Charlottesville, Va.: Albemarle County Historical Society and Theodore Roosevelt Association, 1993); Sylvia Morris, *Edith Kermit Roosevelt,* 289–94.

38. Quoted in Harbaugh, *Pine Knot,* p. 5.

39. Quoted on the dust jacket of Renehan, *Lion's Pride.*

40. Owen Wister, *Roosevelt: The Story of a Friendship, 1880–1919* (New York: Macmillan, 1930), 89.

41. Sylvia Morris, *Edith Kermit Roosevelt,* 287–88.

42. On the Booker T. Washington dinner, see Gatewood, *Art of Controversy,* 32–61; Sylvia Morris, *Edith Kermit Roosevelt,* 227–28; Henry F. Pringle, *Theodore Roosevelt: A Biography* (New York: Harcourt, Brace, 1931), 248–49, with quotations from newspapers.

43. Roosevelt to Edward O. Wolcott, September 5, 1900, in *National Edition,* 14:368–69; Roosevelt, "America and the World War," 1915, ibid., 18:108; *Autobiography,* ibid., 20:491–93. Roosevelt eventually supported independence for the Philippines and Puerto Rico. See Wagenknecht, *Seven Worlds,* 263–64. On imperialism, also see Collin, *Culture, Diplomacy, and Expansion,* chap. 4–epilogue. One of the best studies of Theodore Roosevelt's foreign policy is Frederick W. Marks III, *Velvet on Iron: The Diplomacy of Theodore Roosevelt* (Lincoln: University of Nebraska Press, 1979). Roosevelt's domestic policies represented a democratic nationalism of "Hamiltonian means with Jeffersonian ends," as George E. Mowry says in *Theodore Roosevelt and the Progressive Movement* (Madison: University of Wisconsin Press, 1946), 144–47. Probably the most complete expression of these beliefs was in TR's book *The New Nationalism* (1910), in *National Edition,* ed. Hagedorn, vol. 17. See John

Allen Gable, introd. to Theodore Roosevelt, *The Man in the Arena: Speeches and Essays* (Oyster Bay, N.Y.: Theodore Roosevelt Association, 1987), 1–27; Theodore Roosevelt to George Otto Trevelyan, June 19, 1908, in *Letters,* ed. Morison, Blum, and Chandler, 6:1085–90.

44. Theodore Roosevelt to Henry Cabot Lodge, June 16, 1905, *Letters,* ed. Morison, Blum, and Chandler, 4:1221–33.

45. Theodore Roosevelt to George Otto Trevelyan, June 19, 1908, ibid., 6:1085–90.

46. Theodore Roosevelt to Kermit Roosevelt, January 14, 1909, ibid., 1475–76.

47. Roosevelt's motivations and considerations in running in 1912 were discussed in private conversations with Robert Grant and Otto H. Kahn. See Robert Grant to James Ford Rhodes, March 22, 1912, ibid., vol. 8, app. 2, pp. 1456–61; *Roosevelt As We Knew Him,* ed. Frederick S. Wood (Philadelphia: John C. Winston, 1927), 250–54.

48. Singleton, *Story of the White House,* 2:279. Also see Theodore Roosevelt to Cass Gilbert, December 19, 1908, *Letters,* ed. Morison, Blum, and Chandler, 6:1431; Seale, *President's House,* 722. On TR's high standing with the public and among historians, see "'The Rise of Theodore Roosevelt': TR Rated Highly in New C-SPAN Polls," *Theodore Roosevelt Association Journal* 23, no. 4 (2000): 3–5.

49. Seale, *President's House,* 718.

50. Ethel Roosevelt Derby, conversations with the author in the 1970s. See also "TR and the 'American Century,'" *Theodore Roosevelt Association Journal* 23, no. 2 (1999): 17.

Eleanor Roosevelt about 1933, when she became first lady.

Chapter 10

Eleanor Roosevelt and Franklin Roosevelt
Partnership in Politics and Crises

ALLIDA BLACK

I N the best of times, life in the White House is managed chaos—managed, but chaos, nonetheless. Eleanor Roosevelt and Franklin Roosevelt occupied the White House during the most pressing crises of the twentieth century—the Great Depression and World War II. These crises underscored their shared commitments, exacerbated their political differences, spurred the creation of rival camps within the administration, and encouraged a new public awareness of the role of first lady. How they managed their responsibilities and their differences tells us a great deal about them as a couple, as citizens, and as leaders.

Riding in a day coach to Albany with her aide, the journalist Lorena Hickok, on November 9, 1932, right after the election but before Franklin took office, Eleanor Roosevelt unburdened her thoughts for the record. "I never wanted it even though some people have said that my ambition for myself drove him on. . . . I never wanted to be a President's wife." Fearful that her support for her husband might be misunderstood, she clarified her stance. "For him, of course, I'm glad—sincerely. I could not have wanted it any other way. After all I'm a Democrat, too. Now I shall have to work out my own salvation. I'm afraid it may be a little difficult. I know what Washington is like. I've lived there."[1]

The nation reflected Eleanor Roosevelt's uncertainty. The American press, like the American public, was divided over how professionally active a first lady should be. Criticism of her radio and journalism contracts increased. Suddenly she found herself ridiculed in such diverse publications as the *Harvard Lampoon, Hartford Courant,* and *Baltimore Sun.* By February 1933, the press increasingly interpreted Eleanor's professionalism as rank commercialism. As Lorena Hickok recalled, "All through January and February and right up until March 2, the day they left for Washington, Eleanor continued to do the things she had always done. The papers continued to carry stories about her. And some people continued to criticize her. They just could not get used to the idea of her being 'plain, ordinary Eleanor Roosevelt.'"[2]

Although Eleanor Roosevelt admitted to her friend that she would "curtail somewhat her activities" because she "suppose[d] [she] had made some mistakes," she refused to abandon the expertise she had worked so diligently to achieve. Aware of the criticism her position would provoke, she argued that she had no choice but to continue. "I'll just have to go on being myself, as much as I can. I'm just not the sort of person who would be any good at [any] job. I dare say I shall be criticized, whatever I do."[3]

Eleanor Roosevelt's aversion to a sedentary role was so strong that in the week before the inaugural, she impetuously wrote Marion Dickerman and Nancy Cook that she was contemplating divorcing FDR. She told Hickok, in a quotation for the record, that she "hated" having to resign her teaching position at Todhunter, saying, "I wonder if you have any idea how I hate to do it."[4]

Clearly, when Eleanor Roosevelt entered the White House in March 1933, she did so reluctantly. Her offers to sort FDR's mail and to act as his "listening post" had been rejected summarily. Bowing to his new prestige, she refused to renew her commercial radio contract and resigned as editor of *Babies—Just Babies* when its publisher wanted the magazine to discuss controversial issues in education and child care. Though she tried to avoid it, public expectation was redefining her career and it hurt. "If I wanted to be selfish," she confessed, "I could wish that he had not been elected."[5]

Questions "seethed" in Eleanor's mind about what she should do as first lady. Worried that she would be confined to a schedule of teas and receptions, she tried to create a less restrictive place for herself within the White House. She volunteered to "do a real job" for FDR. During the campaign, she had worked to keep the "channels of communication" between FDR's advisers open, frequently mediating disputes between Louis Howe and Jim Farley. Moreover, she knew that Ettie Rheiner Garner served as an administrative assistant to her husband, the vice president, and Eleanor tried to convince FDR to let her provide the same service. The president rebuffed the first lady's offer. Trapped by convention, she begrudgingly recognized that "the work [was FDR's] work and the pattern his pattern." Disappointed, she acknowledged that she "was one of those who served his purposes."[6]

Nevertheless, Eleanor refused to accept a superficial role. She wanted "to do things on my own, to use my own mind and abilities for my own aims," and she struggled to carve out an active contributory place for herself in the New Deal.

President Franklin D. Roosevelt, 1933, in the Oval Office.

This was not to be a challenge easily met. She found it "hard to remember that I was not just 'Eleanor Roosevelt,' but the 'wife of the President.'"[7]

From her first days in the White House, this desire to remain part of the public action propelled Eleanor Roosevelt's New Deal persona. More often than not, she greeted guests at the door of the White House herself. She learned to operate the White House elevator and adamantly refused Secret Service protection. There also were signs that she intended to be a serious contributor to the Roosevelt administration. She converted the larger room in the Lincoln Bedroom suite into a sitting room and had a telephone installed. She urged the administration to appoint women to positions of influence throughout the New Deal programs. And when the Washington Press Corps refused to admit women members to the annual Gridiron dinner, she gleefully threw herself into planning a "Gridiron Widows" banquet and skit for women officials and reporters.[8]

Concerned that the Federal Emergency Relief Administration (FERA) programs did not meet enough of people's needs, she pressured FERA administrator Harry Hopkins to hire Hickok to tour different parts of the nation, observe FERA programs, and report to him on their effectiveness. Hickok sent copies of these honest, harsh field reports to Eleanor daily, confirming the many obstacles those seeking relief encountered.[9]

When Eleanor read Hickok's accounts of the squalid conditions in the West Virginia coal town of Scott's Run, she was appalled. She met with Louis Howe and Secretary of the Interior Harold Ickes to argue that the Subsistence Homestead provision of the National Industrial Recovery Act should address the community's problems. After winning the argument, she played an active role in designing the housing and became a frequent visitor to the new community, Arthurdale. There she was photographed square-dancing with miners in worn clothes and holding sick children in her lap. This image, when linked with her strong commitment to building the best living quarters the funds could provide, served as a lightning rod for critics of the New Deal, and they delighted in exposing each cost overrun and each program defect.[10]

Eleanor had developed a few close friendships with some of the women who covered her campaign activities, and, with Hickok's and their advice, she eventually turned this media attention to her own advantage. On March 6, two days after her husband became president, Eleanor held her own press conference to announce that she would "get together" with women reporters once a week. She asked for the reporters' cooperation. She hoped that together they could not only discuss her duties as first lady but also explain "what goes on politically in the leg-

Eleanor Roosevelt visiting citizens who would live in Arthurdale, the planned community she sponsored in West Virginia.

islative national life" and encourage women to become active in the New Deal programs in their communities. "The idea," she said, "largely is to make an understanding between the White House and the general public."[11]

Initially Eleanor tried to weight the news discussions toward her traditional social duties and away from her views of the problems the nation confronted. However, as she expanded her role, the topics covered during the press conferences also expanded. Political issues soon became a central part of the weekly briefings. When some members of her press corps tried to caution her to speak off the record, she responded that she knew some of her statements would "cause unfavorable comment in some quarters . . . [but] I am making these statements on purpose to arouse controversy and thereby get the topics talked about."[12]

Recognizing political capital when he saw it, Franklin endorsed Howe's proposal to make Eleanor the administration's roving "ambassador." Within three months, Eleanor had logged 40,000 miles; she traveled so extensively that she drew attention when she remained in Washington. Her observations during these tours only reinforced the impressions she had formed during the final days of the campaign. She returned to Washington convinced that relief programs alone could not counteract the Great Depression and that basic economic reforms were essential. She began to share these views with the women assigned to cover her.

By May she discussed the White House protocol for serving beer—post-Prohibition—her opposition to sweatshops and child labor, the problems confronting those living in the Bonus Army encampment and poverty-stricken Appalachia, and her support for the Veterans National Liaison Committee and higher salaries for teachers. By early June she proclaimed that "very few women know how to read the newspapers," argued that they should pay close attention to international economic news, and delivered a tutorial on how "a busy woman" could keep track of the news "at a time when every one of us ought to be on toes."[13]

By 1934 Eleanor's press conferences became one of the major ways she defended her own activity and the programs Franklin proposed and she championed. Although she never issued a formal statement to the reporters and met with the press only to answer their questions, she soon learned to use these conferences as way to appeal directly to the people. As Bess Furman later recalled, "At the President's press conference, all the world's a stage, at Mrs. Roosevelt's, all the world's a school. . . . Give Mrs. Roosevelt a roomful of newspaper women, and she conducts classes on scores of subjects, always seeing beyond her immediate hearers to the 'women of the country.'"[14]

Eleanor was not satisfied with just disseminating information. She also wanted

Aboard the Amberjack II *sailing from Marion, Massachusetts, to Campobello Island, Nova Scotia, June 16, 1933.*

to know how the public responded to the positions she advocated and those positions promoted by FDR's major critics, Huey Long and Father Charles Coughlin. Consequently, when *Woman's Home Companion* asked her to write a monthly column, she gladly accepted. Announcing that she would donate her monthly thousand-dollar fee to charity, Eleanor then proceeded to ask her readers to help her establish "a clearinghouse, a discussion room" for "the particular problems which puzzle you or sadden you" and to share "how you are adjusting yourself to new conditions in this amazing changing world." Entitling the article "I Want You to Write to Me," she reinforced the request throughout the piece. "Do not hesitate," she wrote in August 1933, "to write to me even if your views clash with what you believe to be my views." Only a free exchange of ideas and discussion of problems would help her "learn of experiences which may be helpful to others." By January 1934, 300,000 Americans responded to this solicitation, more than the total number of letters received by Abraham Lincoln and Woodrow Wilson in their first year in office and equal to the weekly circulation of Long's *American Progress.*[15]

This was not a token offer. Eleanor had personal and political reasons for appealing for public input. Worried that Long and Coughlin supporters felt neglected by the New Deal, she wanted to make herself available to them. Yet her appeal to the public was not motivated solely by her dissatisfaction. Her commitment to free and unrestricted public discussion was heartfelt and intense. She considered the free exchange of information and ideas central to democracy's success. The more informed the public was about the issues it confronted, the more educated the society would become, and the more opportunities democracy would have to be realized.

When she entered the White House, Eleanor believed that recovery could not happen unless all America took responsibility for correcting the economic problems that had pushed the nation into the Depression. Legislation alone could not solve the problems. What the country needed desperately was "some new changes in our rather settled ideas." Moreover, those who avoided personal commitment by claiming that no one would listen to their demands, she told "My Day" readers in 1935, were promoting a civic "inferiority complex" to provide themselves with "a comfortable alibi to side step responsibility."[16]

From her first days in the White House, this conviction propelled Eleanor Roosevelt's New Deal agenda. While Franklin Roosevelt shared some of these beliefs, he did not actively promote them until late 1935, with the legislation most commonly associated with what historians have labeled the Second New Deal. Consequently, Eleanor Roosevelt's first policy task as first lady was to prod her

Eleanor Roosevelt at a White House garden party for soldiers, 1942.

husband to incorporate as generous a definition of minimum economic security and social welfare as politically possible. While most historians view Eleanor's commitment to Arthurdale as the best example of her influence within the New Deal, this assessment is too one-dimensional to reflect the breadth of her commitment to democratic reform. She did more than champion a single antipoverty program. Continuously she urged that relief should be as diverse as the constituency that needed it.

"The unemployed are not a strange race. They are like we would be if we had not had a fortunate chance at life," Eleanor wrote in 1936. The distress they encountered, not their socioeconomic status, should be the focus of relief. Consequently, she introduced programs for groups not originally included in New Deal plans; supported others that were in danger of elimination or having their funds cut; pushed the hiring of women, African Americans, and liberals within federal agencies; and acted as the administration's most outspoken champion of liberal reform.[17]

Eleanor did not immediately begin to push programs. Rather, as her actions to modify the Federal Emergency Relief Administration and the Civil Works Administration (CWA) show, she waited to see how the programs FDR's aides designed were put into operation and then lobbied for improvements or suggested alternatives. When the needs of unemployed women were overlooked by FERA and CWA planners, she lobbied first to have women's divisions established within both agencies and then to have specific women appointed as program directors. She then planned and chaired the White House Conference on the Emergency Needs of Women and monitored the Household Workers' Training Program that was established during the conference.[18]

Eleanor addressed the problems of unemployed youth with the same fervor she applied to women's economic hardships. This, also, was not a politically popular position for her to take. The unemployed youth of the 1930s underscored several fears adults had for society. Conservatives, fearing duplication of the radicalism spreading among European youth, saw disgruntled young people as a fertile ground for revolutionary politics. Progressives mourned disillusionment and apathy that seemed to be spreading among the young. But Eleanor thought that camps in the Civilian Conservation Corps, while providing temporary relief for some youth, did not meet their needs. Furthermore, because the camps were supervised by military personnel and provided instruction only in forestry, she believed that an additional program tailored to the special needs of youth was urgently needed. In mid-1933 she pressured Harry Hopkins to develop a program for youth that would provide a social rather than a militaristic focus. She argued that the specific problems facing youth needed to be recognized, but only in a way that fostered a sense of self-worth. By providing job skills and education, she hoped that the program would foster a sense of civic awareness that in turn would promote a commitment to social justice. Then youth would be empowered to articulate their own needs and aspirations and to express these insights clearly.

Although historians disagree over how major a role Eleanor played in creating the National Youth Administration (NYA), her imprint upon the agency's development is indelible. Established by an executive order signed by the president on June 26, 1935, the NYA was authorized to administer programs in five areas: work projects, vocational guidance, apprenticeship training, educational and nutritional guidance camps for unemployed women, and student aid. Clearly Eleanor's preference for vocational guidance and education triumphed over the CCC relief model. Moreover, Eleanor was both the agency's and youth's natural choice for confessor, planner, lobbyist, and promoter. She reviewed NYA policy with agency directors, arranged for NYA officials and youth leaders to meet with FDR in and out of the White House, served as NYA's intermediary with the president, critiqued and suggested projects, and attended as many NYA state administrators' conferences as her schedule allowed. Last but not least, she visited at least 112 NYA sites and reported her observations in her speeches, articles, and "My Day," the daily column she began in 1935. Eleanor took such satisfaction in the NYA that when she briefly acknowledged her role in forming the agency, she did so with an uncharacteristic candor. "One of the ideas I agreed to present to Franklin," she wrote in *This I Remember,* "was that of setting up a national youth administration.... It was one of the occasions on which I was very proud that the right thing was done regardless of political consequences."[19]

Besides listening to the concerns of youth, Eleanor also met with unemployed artists and writers to discuss their concerns. They asked for her support for a public arts program. She agreed immediately and attended the preliminary planning meeting. Sitting at the head table next to Edward Bruce, the meeting's organizer, Eleanor knitted while she listened to Bruce propose a program to pay artists for creating public art. Advocating a program in which artists could control both form and content, Bruce recruited supporters for federally financed work appropriate for public buildings. Sitting quietly through most of the discussion, Eleanor interrupted only to question procedure and to emphasize her support of the project.[20]

Eleanor became the Public Works Arts Project's (PWAP) ardent public and private champion. When PWAP artists were sent to Civil Conservation Corps camps in mid-1934 and produced more than two hundred watercolors, oil paint-ings, and chalk drawings portraying camp life, she enthusiastically opened their "Life in the CCC" exhibit at the National Museum. When five hundred PWAP artworks were displayed at Washington's Corcoran Gallery, she dedicated the ex-hibit and declared that in addition to its artistic merit, the works liberated society greatly by expressing what many people could find no words to describe.[21]

After Bruce was appointed PWAP director, he proposed that artists be eligible for Works Progress Administration (WPA) programs. Immediately he solicited Eleanor's support. She agreed that artists were in need of government aid and sup-ported the WPA venture, in the process entering the internal dispute over whether FERA should fund white-collar programs. With the support of FERA administra-tor Harry Hopkins, Eleanor lobbied Franklin to endorse Bruce's concept. The president agreed, issuing an executive order on June 25, 1935, that created the Fed-eral One Programs of the Works Progress Administration: the Federal Writers Pro-ject, the Federal Theater Project, and the Federal Art Project (formerly PWAP).

PLATE 15

Eleanor Roosevelt continued to run administrative interference after the pro-grams were in operation. When Jean Baker, director of the WPA Professional and Service Products Division, gave in to pressure from conservatives who wanted to place the program under local control, Eleanor convinced Hopkins that Baker should be replaced. Hopkins agreed and filled Baker's post with Eleanor's close friend Ellen Woodward. Eleanor also continued to promote the project despite its increas-ingly controversial image. When Hallie Flanagan asked for assistance in convincing Congress that the Federal Theater Project was not a heretical attack on American culture, Eleanor agreed on the spot. The first lady told Flanagan that she would gladly go to Capitol Hill because the time had come when America must recognize that art is controversial and the controversy is an important part of education.[22]

Despite the fervor with which ER campaigned for a more democratic ad-ministration of relief through the establishment of women's divisions, NYA, and the three Federal One programs, these efforts paled in comparison to the unceas-ing pressure she placed upon the president and the nation to confront the eco-nomic and political discrimination faced by black America. Although the first lady did not become an ardent proponent of racial integration until the 1950s, through-out the 1930s and 1940s she nevertheless persistently labeled racial prejudice as un-democratic and immoral. Black Americans recognized the depth of her commitment and consequently kept faith with FDR because his wife kept faith with them.

Eleanor's racial policies attracted notice almost immediately. Less than a week after becoming first lady, she surprised conservative Washington society by announcing that the White House would have an entirely African American domestic staff. By late summer 1933, photographs appeared showing her discussing living conditions with black miners in West Virginia, and the press treated her involvement in the antilynching campaign as front-page news. Rumors of Eleanor's "race-baiting" actions sped across the South with hurricane force. But Eleanor refused to be intimidated by rumor. She mobilized cabinet and congressional wives for a walking tour of Washington's slum alleys to increase support for slum clearance and low-cost housing legislation then before Congress. After being intensively briefed by Walter White she toured the Virgin Islands with Lorena Hickok in 1934, investigating conditions for herself only to return agreeing with White's initial assessments. In 1935 she visited Howard University's Freedmen's Hospital, lobbied Congress for increased appropriations, and praised the institution in her press conferences. Franklin's disapproval kept her from attending the 1934 and 1935 National Association for the Advancement of Colored People (NAACP) conventions, but his cautiousness did not affect her support of the organization. Indeed, she telegraphed her deep disappointment to the delegates and then joined the local chapter of the NAACP and National Urban League, becoming the first white Washington resident to respond to the membership drives. And, in contrast to Franklin, who refrained from actively supporting antilynching legislation, a very public Eleanor refused to leave the Senate gallery during the filibuster over the bill.[23]

As the 1936 election approached, Eleanor continued her inspections and finally convinced Franklin to let her address the NAACP and National Urban League annual conventions. When the *New Yorker* published the famous cartoon of miners awaiting her visit, she aggressively defended her outreach to minorities and the poor in a lengthy article for the *Saturday Evening Post*. She attacked those directly who mocked her interest. "In strange and subtle ways," she began, "it was indicated to me that I should feel ashamed of that cartoon and that there was certainly something the matter with a woman who wanted to see so much and know so much." She refused to be so limited and responded to those "blind" critics whom she thought refused to be interested in anything outside their own four walls.[24]

The liberal and conservative press gave such action prominent coverage. When Eleanor addressed the National Urban League's annual convention, NBC radio nationally broadcast the address. When she visited Howard University and was escorted around campus by its Honor Guard, the *Georgia Woman's World* printed a photograph of the event on its front page while castigating the first lady for conduct unbecoming to a president's wife. Mainstream media such as the *New York Times* and *Christian Science Monitor* questioned the extent to which Eleanor would be "a campaign issue."[25]

Eleanor Roosevelt increased her civil rights activism in her second term as first lady. She continued her outspoken advocacy of antilynching legislation, served as an active co-chair of the National Committee to Abolish the Poll Tax, spoke out in favor of National Sharecropper's Week, urged Agricultural Adjustment Act administrators to recognize the discriminatory practices of white landowners, pressured FERA administrators to pay black and white workers equal salaries, and invited black guests and entertainers to the White House. With an NYA administrator, Mary McLeod Bethune, she convened the National Conference of Negro Women at the White House and publicized the agenda that the conference promoted. She also pressured the Resettlement Administration to recognize that black sharecroppers' problems deserved their attention and lent her active endorsement to the Southern Conference on Human Welfare (SCHW).

Often the public stances Eleanor Roosevelt took were more effective than the lobbying she did behind the scenes. When she entered the SCHW's 1938 convention in Birmingham, Alabama, police officers told her that she would not be allowed to sit with Bethune because a city ordinance outlawed integrated seating. Eleanor then requested a chair and placed it squarely between the aisles, highlighting her displeasure with Jim Crow policies. In February 1939 she resigned from the Daughters of the American Revolution when the organization refused to rent its auditorium to the internationally known black contralto Marian Anderson.[26] Eleanor then announced her decision in her newspaper column, thereby transforming a local act into a national disgrace. When Howard University students picketed neighborhood lunch stands that denied them service, Eleanor praised their courage and sent them money to continue their public education programs. And when A. Philip Randolph and other civil rights leaders threatened to march on Washington unless FDR acted to outlaw discrimination in defense industries, Eleanor took their demands home to the White House.[27]

By the early 1940s Eleanor Roosevelt firmly believed the civil rights issue to be the real litmus test for American democracy. Thus, she declared over and over again throughout the war that there could be no democracy in the United States that did not include democracy for blacks. In *The Moral Basis of Democracy* (1940), she asserted that people of all races have inviolate rights to property. "We have never been willing to face this problem, to line it up with the basic, underlying beliefs in Democracy." Racial prejudice enslaved blacks; consequently, "no one can claim that . . . the Negroes of this country are free." She continued this theme in a 1942 article in the *New Republic,* declaring that both the private and the public sector must acknowledge that "one of the main destroyers of freedom is our attitude toward the colored race." "What Kipling called 'The White Man's Burden,'" she proclaimed in the *American Magazine,* is "one of the things we can not have any longer." Furthermore, she told those listening to the radio broadcast of the 1945 National Democratic forum, "Democracy may grow or fade as we face [this] problem."[28]

When, during World War II, Eleanor dared to equate American racism with fascism and argued that to ignore the evils of segregation would be capitulating to Aryanism, hostility against her reached an all-time high. Newspapers from Chicago to Louisiana covered the dispute, and numerous citizens pleaded with J. Edgar Hoover, director of the Federal Bureau of Investigation, to silence her. Refusing to concede to her opponents, she continuously asserted that if the nation continued to honor Jim Crow, America would have defeated fascism abroad only to defend racism at home.[29]

The Anderson experience reinforced Eleanor's venture into the politics of confrontation and helped steel her for the 1940 campaign. Although the first lady was no stranger to criticism by April 1939, the strong and widespread reaction her endorsement of Anderson generated was a new experience for her. By fall she had become the Republicans' most popular target, and attacks she discounted in public as "mudslinging" became so intense, she wrote her aunt, that "the campaign is as bad in personal bitterness as any I have ever been in."[30]

But Eleanor's influence within the party held fast. When FDR's choice for vice president, Henry Wallace, unquestionably the most liberal member of FDR's cabinet, was in jeopardy, Franklin called Eleanor and asked her to fly to the convention and salvage Wallace's candidacy. Earlier that day, Ickes frantically telegraphed FDR that the "convention is bleeding to death." Delegates needed more direction from him. They were "milling around like worried sheep." FDR had alienated delegates by insisting that he would respond only to a draft (thereby refusing to ask for their support directly); and after they had swallowed their pride and renominated him, the convention fractured over the issue of his running mate. Furthermore, the candidate FDR wanted had just left the Republican party. Chaos reigned in the Chicago convention hall when Eleanor Roosevelt arrived. She later

IFORNIA

recalled that when Wallace's name was placed in nomination, the noise generated by the various floor fights was so "deafening" that "you could hardly hear yourself or speak to your next door neighbor."[31]

No first lady had ever addressed a national political convention and Malvina ("Tommy") Thompson, Eleanor's secretary and valued confidante, adamantly opposed her boss's appearance. Thompson was not Eleanor's only friend who worried that she "would be sacrificed on the altar of hysteria." Even Frances Perkins and Lorena Hickok, the two who had convinced Eleanor to come to Chicago, panicked at the disorder reigning beneath the speaker's podium and urged the chair to delay her address. But Eleanor discounted their panic and strode across the dais. Her appearance not only stopped the floor fights but also ignited a passionate, spontaneous demonstration in her honor that surpassed even the sustained applause Jim Farley had received the night before, when he had used his nomination speech to ask the delegates to unite behind Roosevelt.

Briefly pausing to acknowledge their praise, Eleanor then began to speak, without notes, to the Democratic crowd below her. Without mentioning Wallace by name, she appealed to the delegates to give the president the help he asked of them. Reminding them that "no man who is a candidate or who is President can carry this situation alone," she asked them to remember that "this is no ordinary time" and that "we have no time for weighing anything except what we can best do for the country as a whole."[32]

Wallace received the necessary votes on the first ballot. Eleanor's skillful, dramatic rebuttal of the delegates' challenge to Wallace's nomination for vice president in 1940 received banner headlines across the land. Party regulars considered her speech to the Democratic National Con-

Eleanor Roosevelt addressing the Democratic Convention in Chicago, July 18, 1940.

vention a masterstroke. Her performance, the quintessential progressive George Norris wrote, made her "the Sheridan of that convention [who] caused men of sense and honor to stop and think before they plunged." Only Eleanor's deft handling of the delegates, the senator concluded, "turned a rout into a victory." Sam Rosenman, FDR's adviser who sat with the president in his White House study listening to the address over the radio, agreed. She had managed to lift the convention "above the petty political trading that was going on and place it on a different level."[33]

Nor were such voices heard solely from outside her own circle. Frequently, FDR's immediate concerns dictated not only the topics Eleanor examined but the extent of the action she could undertake. Often his friends objected to her influence. Doc O'Connor and Sam Rosenman, FDR's legal advisers, told Rexford Tugwell when he joined the 1932 campaign team that their first task was "to get the pants off Eleanor and onto Frank." Many New Deal officials, like Secretary of Labor Frances Perkins, disapproved of her civil rights employment policies and feared the response they would provoke from southern congressional leaders. Secretary of the Interior Harold L. Ickes resented Eleanor's participation in the development of the subsistence homestead in Arthurdale, West Virginia, and feared being upstaged within the civil rights community. Others, like the secretary of agriculture, feared her power within the administration. "Now, Will, I want to give you some advice," Henry Wallace told his newly appointed Farm Security administrator, Will Alexander, "You want to let that woman alone. She's a very dangerous person. You don't want to get mixed up with her." And as numerous historians have reported, when FDR became preoccupied with winning the world war, Eleanor's insistent focus on domestic issues irritated the president, angered his advisers, and provoked outrage from conservative members of Congress. By the time FDR sought a fourth term in 1944, the Roosevelts' divergent politics were blatantly apparent.[34]

Thus, even within the confines of the White House family quarters, politics was not always compromise but often confrontation. Advocates of each opposing view joined ranks and justified their positions by arguing that their individual packages for more broad-based reform were more important than any single policy. No stranger to political arbitration, Eleanor sometimes won these contests. However, when she lost, she did not concede defeat easily. A skilled and committed player, she studied the rules and continued playing. As Rexford Tugwell, one of the original members of FDR's Brain Trust, described Eleanor Roosevelt's powerful attempts to modify her husband's agenda, "No one who ever saw Eleanor Roosevelt sit down facing her husband, and, holding his eye firmly, say to him, 'Franklin, I think you should . . .' or, 'Franklin, surely you will not . . .' will ever forget the experience." With the vigilance of a wrangler riding herd, she spurred the administration's side "even though the spurring was not always wanted or welcome." "It would be impossible," Tugwell concluded, "to say how often and to what extent American governmental processes have been turned in new directions because of her determination."[35]

"She had this sense of having to do whatever was humanly possible in a difficult time," recalled Trude Lash, who had met Mrs. Roosevelt as a youth worker. Her energy was so intense that a standard joke of the day was "Please, Lord, make Eleanor tired." Author, columnist, politician, and educator, this woman appeared indefatigable. From 1933 to 1945, she wrote, without a ghostwriter, more than 2,500 columns, published six books and more than two hundred articles, and delivered at least seventy speeches a year. She lobbied for legislation, advised politicians and reformers, met with Democratic Party leaders, and traveled the country as her husband's representative.[36]

Eleanor and Franklin Roosevelt formed a political partnership unique in American history. Its uniqueness stemmed not only from its composition but from the backdrop it was set against. Eleanor did not want to be first lady, and Franklin did not want her to be involved in administration policy or politics. But the thirteen years Eleanor spent in the White House redefined the role so dramatically that she set the standard against which most of her successors have been judged. Her skillful use of the media (as columnist, subject, and radio personality) not only increased Franklin's political clout but often also provided him necessary political "cover" as well as goading him to address issues he would rather have postponed.

Just as this was "no ordinary time," the Roosevelt partnership was no ordinary collaboration. Their relationship was strengthened by commitment to the nation, a partnership often fraught with divergent convictions and priorities, yet an alliance essential to national morale in times of crisis.

NOTES

1. Quoted in Lorena Hickok, *Eleanor Roosevelt: Reluctant First Lady* (New York: Dodd, Mead, 1962), 2–3; Hickok, Associated Press News Copy, New York, November 9–11, 1932, box 14, Lorena Hickok Papers, Franklin D. Roosevelt Library, Hyde Park, New York.

2. Hickok, *Reluctant First Lady,* 87; also see Associated Press News Copy, New York, February 4, 1933, Hickok Papers, Roosevelt Library. For examples of articles supporting Eleanor Roosevelt's

activities, see "Mrs. Roosevelt's Vocation," *Wheeling (West Virginia) Register,* December 29, 1932; untitled editorial in *Albany (Ga.) Herald,* January 14, 1933; *Baltimore Evening Sun,* February 4, 1932; *Hartford Courant,* quoted in "Mrs. Roosevelt's Activities," *Springfield (Mass.) Evening News,* December 22, 1932. For articles criticizing Eleanor's actions, see "Mrs. Roosevelt Has Many Jobs," *Selma (Ala.) Times-Journal,* December 22, 1932, and other clippings. Miscellaneous Clippings Related to Eleanor Roosevelt, 1929–32, Anna Eleanor Roosevelt papers, Roosevelt Library.

3. Quoted in Hickok, Associated Press News Copy, New York, February 4, 1933, Hickok Papers; Maurine Beasley, *Eleanor Roosevelt and the Media* (Urbana: University of Illinois Press, 1987), 34; Hickok, *Reluctant First Lady,* 85, 87; "Mrs. Roosevelt to Abandon Many Activities in March," clipping, February 5, 1933, Miscellaneous Newspaper Clippings Related to Eleanor Roosevelt, 1933–45, Eleanor Roosevelt Papers.

4. Quoted in Hickok, *Reluctant First Lady,* 3; Hickok, Associated Press News Copy, New York, November 11, 1932, box 14, Hickok Papers.

5. Quoted in Allida Black, *Casting Her Own Shadow: Eleanor Roosevelt and the Shaping of Postwar Liberalism, 1945–1962* (New York: Columbia University Press, 1996), 20–22. See also Hickok, *Reluctant First Lady,* chap. 8.

6. Eleanor Roosevelt, *This I Remember* (New York: Harper & Brothers, 1949), 76.

7. Ibid., 76, 89.

8. Blanche Wiesen Cook, *Eleanor Roosevelt: A Life* (New York: Viking, 1999), 2:33, 47.

9. See Richard Lowitt and Maurine Beasley, *One Third of a Nation: Lorena Hickok Reports on the Great Depression* (Urbana: University of Illinois Press, 1986), for the complete correspondence.

10. Cook, *Eleanor Roosevelt: A Life,* 2:130–53; Joseph P. Lash, *Eleanor and Franklin* (New York: W. W. Norton, 1970), chap. 37; Lois Scharf, *Eleanor Roosevelt: First Lady of American Liberalism* (Boston: Twayne, 1987), 102–3; William Leuchtenburg, *Franklin D. Roosevelt and the New Deal* (New York: Harper & Row, 1963), 136–37, 185; Arthur M. Schlesinger Jr., *The Coming of the New Deal* (Boston: Houghton Mifflin, 1959), 366–67; and Frank Freidel, *FDR: Launching the New Deal* (Boston: Little, Brown, 1973), 296–97. Eleanor Roosevelt to Bernard Baruch, June 13, 1934, Personal Correspondence, Eleanor Roosevelt Papers.

11. Eleanor Roosevelt, *This I Remember,* 76, 80–82; Lorena Hickok, "Nation's 'First Lady' Outlines Plans As She Begins White House Residence," *New York Times,* March 5, 1933; Bess Furman, *Washington By-Line* (New York: Alfred A. Knopf, 1949), 150–52; Beasley, *Eleanor Roosevelt and the Media,* 51–67.

12. Eleanor Roosevelt, interview by Emma Bugbee, quoted in Lash, *Eleanor and Franklin,* 363.

13. For Eleanor's comments on political issues, see Eleanor Roosevelt, *The White House Press Conferences of Eleanor Roosevelt,* ed. Maurine Beasley (New York: Garland Publishing, 1983), 6–9.

14. Ibid., 67; Furman, *Washington By-Line,* 194.

15. Eleanor Roosevelt, "I Want You to Write to Me," *Woman's Home Companion,* August 1933, 4; Eleanor Roosevelt, "Mail of a President's Wife," unpublished article, ca. 1939, Speech and Article File, Eleanor Roosevelt Papers; Alan Brinkley, *Voices of Protest: Huey Long, Father Coughlin and the Great Depression* (New York: Vintage, 1983), 70. For an extensive discussion of Eleanor's attitude about her mail, see Frances M. Seeber, "'I Want You to Write to Me': The Papers of Anna Eleanor Roosevelt," *Prologue* 19, no. 2 (Summer 1987): 95–105.

16. Eleanor Roosevelt, "Chautauqua Speech," July 12, 1932, Speech and Article File, Eleanor

Roosevelt Papers; *New York Times,* January 12, 1933, July 26, 1935; Eleanor Roosevelt, "My Day," March 17, 1936, My Day Collection, Eleanor Roosevelt Papers. "My Day" was first published December 31, 1935.

17. Eleanor Roosevelt, "The Unemployed Are Not a Strange Race," *Democratic Digest* 13, no. 6 (June 1936): 19, reprinted in *What I Hope to Leave Behind: The Essential Essays of Eleanor Roosevelt,* ed. Allida Black (Brooklyn: Carlson Publishing, 1994), 367.

18. Black, *Casting Her Own Shadow,* 28–30.

19. Ibid., 30–33; Roosevelt, *This I Remember,* 162–63.

20. Olin Downes, "The New Deal's Treasury Art Program: A Memoir," in *New Deal Art Projects: An Anthology of Memoirs,* ed. Francis V. O'Connor (Washington, D.C.: Smithsonian Institution Press, 1972); William F. MacDonald, *Federal Relief Administration of the Arts* (Columbus: Ohio State University Press, 1969), 363; Richard D. McKinzie, *The New Deal for Artists* (Princeton, N.J.: Princeton University Press, 1973), 10.

21. Eleanor Roosevelt, "The New Governmental Interest in Art," Speech and Article File, Eleanor Roosevelt Papers, reprinted in *Courage in a Dangerous World: The Political Writings of Eleanor Roosevelt,* ed. Allida Black (New York: Columbia University Press, 1999), 26–28; Downes, "New Deal's Treasury Art Program"; Edward Lansing, "The New Deal Mural Projects," in *The New Deal Art Projects,* ed. O'Connor, 105; James Michael Newell, interview ibid.

22. Black, *Casting Her Own Shadow,* 33–36.

23. Ibid., 38; Walter White to Eleanor Roosevelt, August 28, 1934, and Eleanor Roosevelt to Walter White, September 7, 1934, Personal Correspondence, Eleanor Roosevelt Papers; *Press Conferences of Eleanor Roosevelt,* ed. Beasley, 42–44, 49; Eleanor Roosevelt to Walter White, June 15, 1935, Personal Correspondence, Eleanor Roosevelt Papers; Nancy J. Weiss, *Farewell to the Party of Lincoln: Black Politics in the Age of FDR* (Princeton, N.J.: Princeton University Press, 1983), 126.

24. Eleanor Roosevelt, "In Defense of Curiosity," *Saturday Evening Post* 208 (August 24, 1935): 8, reprinted in *Courage in a Dangerous World,* ed. Black; Eleanor Roosevelt, "Responsibility to Fellow Human Beings," Speech and Article file, Eleanor Roosevelt Papers.

25. Black, *Casting Her Own Shadow,* 38; Eleanor Roosevelt, "The Negro and Social Change," *Opportunity: The Journal of Negro Life,* January 1936, 22; the *Georgia Women's World* piece is referred to in a *New York Times,* November 8, 1936, clipping in Miscellaneous Clippings, Eleanor Roosevelt Papers; M. Hornaday, "Mrs. Roosevelt, a Campaign Issue," *Christian Science Monitor,* June 24, 1936, 5; and editorial, *Baltimore Afro-American,* May 23, 1936, 4.

26. The Anderson controversy taught Eleanor Roosevelt a valuable lesson. She clearly saw the impact she had when she used her column for political persuasion. In 1939 she was just beginning to use "My Day" as her own political forum. The Marian Anderson controversy and the response it generated from her readers showed her the direct impact she had when she spoke out on a political event. She received more mail supporting her resignation from the DAR than she did on any other issue she associated herself with in 1939. Gallup and other public opinion polls revealed that her backing of Anderson increased her popularity in all areas of the country except the deep South, and even there, the decrease was minuscule. Eleanor did not overlook the political and organizational lessons this event taught her about coalition building and the power of her column. Although "My Day" continued to be primarily an insight into the first lady's personal schedule, by mid-July 1939 she recognized the political power she could muster in her own right for an issue she chose

to highlight. In April 1940 United Feature Syndicate acknowledged her appeal by awarding her a five-year renewal for "My Day" at a time when Franklin's reelection plans were not known.

27. Black, *Casting Her Own Shadow,* 84–91.

28. Eleanor Roosevelt, *The Moral Basis of Democracy* (New York: Howell, Soskin, 1940), 48; "The Issue Is Freedom," *New Republic,* August 3, 1942, 147–48; draft, "What Are We Fighting For?" *American Magazine,* July 1942; "Broadcast: National Democratic Forum," February 24, 1945, Speech and Article File, Eleanor Roosevelt Papers.

29. Black, *Casting Her Own Shadow,* 88–96.

30. Eleanor Roosevelt to Maude Gray, October 17, 1940, quoted in Lash, *Eleanor and Franklin,* 629.

31. Frances Perkins interview, Oral History Research Office, Columbia University; Eleanor Roosevelt interview, Graff Papers, Roosevelt Library; *Washington Post,* July 19, 1940; Doris Kearns Goodwin, *No Ordinary Time: Franklin and Eleanor Roosevelt, The Home Front in World War II* (New York: Simon & Schuster, 1994), 130–33; *New York Times,* July 19, 1940.

32. Speech quoted in full in *New York Times,* July 19, 1940.

33. George Norris to Eleanor Roosevelt, July 19, 1940, Personal Correspondence, Eleanor Roosevelt Papers. For a thorough discussion of Eleanor's role at the convention, see R. S. Kirkendall, "ER and the Issue of FDR's Successor," in *The Life and Career of Eleanor Roosevelt,* ed. Joan Hoff and Marjorie Lightman (Bloomington: Indiana University Press, 1984), 178–80; Lash, *Eleanor and Franklin,* 622–25; Joseph Lash, *Eleanor Roosevelt: A Friend's Memoir* (New York: Doubleday, 1964), 131–39; Frances Perkins, *The Roosevelt I Knew* (New York: Viking Press, 1946); Jim Farley, *Jim Farley's Story* (New York: McGraw-Hill, 1948), 299–307; and Goodwin, *No Ordinary Time.* Farley wrote that Eleanor supported Jesse Jones over Henry Wallace because Jones would bolster business support and increase party contributions. She disputed this. "I expressed no preference for any candidate and I think the account of the convention which Jim Farley gave in his book . . . was his impression of what I said rather than what I actually said." Eleanor Roosevelt, *This I Remember,* 216.

34. Rexford Tugwell, *The Brains Trust* (New York: Macmillan, 1968), 54. Alexander refused to take this advice and, when reviewing his experiences in Washington, wrote, "I . . . trusted Mrs. Roosevelt [and her judgment] more than anybody I ever saw." Ickes recorded his displeasure with the first lady in his diary: "I am very fond of Eleanor Roosevelt. She has a fine social sense and is utterly selfless, but as the President has said to me on one or two occasions, she wants to build these homesteads on a scale that we can't afford because the people for whom they are intended cannot afford such homes. The President's idea is to build an adequate house and not even put in plumbing fixtures, leaving that sort of thing to be done later by the homesteader as he can afford them. He remarked yesterday that he had not yet dared say this to the people (undoubtedly meaning Eleanor Roosevelt) who wanted the houses built with all modern improvements." Harold L. Ickes, *The Secret Diary of Harold L. Ickes* (New York: Doubleday, 1953), 1:227. For an extensive account of Mrs. Roosevelt's commitment to the Arthurdale project, see Lash, *Eleanor and Franklin,* chap. 38. Alexander recounts his conversation with Wallace in his unfinished biography, "A Southern Rebel," in the Will Alexander Papers, Roosevelt Library.

35. For firsthand accounts of Mrs. Roosevelt's lobbying efforts within the White House and the reasons for her successes and failures, see the following transcripts. Interviewees discuss the division of White House staff into "camps" supporting and opposing Mrs. Roosevelt's efforts. James

Halstead, interview by Emily Williams, May 17 and 22, 1979, transcript, Eleanor Roosevelt Oral History Project (EROHP), Roosevelt Library. Anna Rosenberg Hoffman, interview by Thomas Soapes, October 13, 1977, transcript, EROHP; James Rowe, interview by Emily Williams, July 12, 1978, transcript, EROHP; Jonathan Daniels, interview by Emily Williams, November 16, 1979, EROHP. Eleanor Roosevelt, *This I Remember,* 279; Rexford Tugwell, "Remarks," *Roosevelt Day Dinner Journal,* Americans for Democratic Action, January 31, 1963.

36. Lash, quoted in Goodwin, *No Ordinary Time,* 104.

President Gerald R. Ford inaugurates the new White House swimming pool, July 5, 1975.

Chapter 11

White House
News Photographers and
the White House

D E N N I S   B R A C K

THE White House is an interesting subject for photographs. I will describe the men and women who made these photographs for the news and relate a few stories about the White House and its occupants that have been passed along to me from an earlier generation, mostly in and around the White House News Photographers Association. Both the technology of photography and the news business have changed the way the association's members cover the White House.

At the time of World War I, large military camps sprang up around Washington. Public interest was directed toward the soldiers training in these camps, so to feed this market, the large papers and syndicates began positioning staff photographers in their Washington bureaus. After the war, the major beat of these photographers shifted to the White House.

The final year of the Wilson administration, 1920–21, was a difficult time for White House photographers. Their editors demanded photographs of the feeble President Woodrow Wilson after his stroke. He had become very reclusive; his wife and doctor literally sequestered him. Photographers were not allowed on the White House grounds, much less allowed to photograph the president. The best they could do was stand across West Executive Avenue (it was an open street in those days), run after visitors to the White House, and try to take their pictures. Sometimes they were successful, sometimes not.

But these news photographers were not the type of fellows who were content to stand and wait. A sneak attack was in order. A flock of sheep grazed on the South Lawn. Every morning a load of hay was rolled through the gate for these sheep to munch on. One morning H. M. Van Tine climbed under the hay with his 5 x 7 camera, hoping to get a picture of the elusive President Wilson in his wheelchair.

163

President Warren G. Harding and the White House news corps, May 29, 1921. Harding, a newspaperman himself, was a popular subject for the news photographers and eagerly obliged.

But a Secret Service agent noticed that the hay was a bit lumpy and began poking a stick into the load. Back to the curb. Things had to change, the photographers reasoned. And beginning with the Harding administration, they did. The photographers began to organize, and even the Secret Service hoped, as one put it, "that the picture men would band together."

In 1921 twenty-four photographers (including Van Tine) formed the White House News Photographers Association and gained recognition from George B.

Christian, President Warren G. Harding's secretary. The photographers' big break came when President Harding walked back from lunch and asked about all those men standing along West Executive Avenue. He was told that they were the photographers, and they weren't allowed on the grounds. President Harding, a journalist himself, said that the photographers were journalists just like the reporters and they should be given the same access as the reporters. We were in!

President Harding seemed to enjoy being photographed. Laddy Boy, the president's Airedale, was known by every American, thanks to news photographers' pictures. I guess it was appropriate that Harding had a small wooden hut built on the White House grounds for the photographers, and it later came to be known as the doghouse.

Calvin Coolidge had served a term as vice president and had been called upon to perform many of the duties that the president had no time to do, such as posing for photographs with visiting dignitaries. The photographers trained him well. When he was president, he was never too busy to have his picture taken. One of our members heard someone asking Coolidge what he did for exercise, and the president just pointed to the photographers and said, "I do what the photographers ask me to do and that's plenty of exercise." One photograph records that President Coolidge had enough exercise.

During the 1920s new technology brought changes to news organizations covering the White House. As photographs began to be transmitted by radio and telephone wires, local photographic studios declined and the wire services were founded. Movie newsreels, now with sound, kept the public informed of current events. And the photographers had flash powder. We were lethal. Flash powder was a sprinkle of magnesium in a ten-inch V-shaped metal tray that produced the brilliant light needed to expose the extremely slow film used at that time. The photographers got only one shot because very shortly after that brilliant light came a thick cloud of gray-black dust that settled over everything.

When they did get to take a picture inside the White House, the photographers set their cameras on tripods and pooled their powder. One photographer would say, "Open shutter," and they all would open their camera shutters. The flash powder would be ignited, and each photographer would get the picture at the same instant. Everyone liked it when the president said, "Let's go outside for the photograph."

During the Hoover administration, the photographers needed all the help that they could get. Herbert Hoover was a tough subject. He had a nervous dislike of the cameras. Recently I talked with Johnny di Joseph, age ninety-five, who started

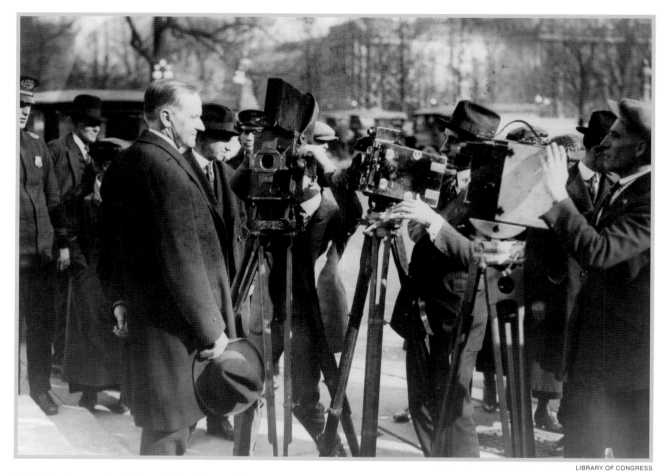

Following the gregarious Warren G. Harding in office, President Calvin Coolidge accommodated news photographers, who had developed quite an appetite for presidents.

taking pictures in Washington in 1917. Coolidge was his favorite president, but when I asked Johnny about President Hoover, he said, "He was okay. It was his wife: she had a rule that no photographer could come within fifteen feet of the president to take a picture." President Hoover always wore two-inch-high collars with his shirts; Johnny called them "horse collars." The first lady didn't like the way his double chins fell over these stiff white collars, and she thought that keeping the photographers fifteen feet away would prevent them from making close-up photographs of her husband.

The Franklin D. Roosevelt years brought new tools and new rules. The 4 x 5 Speed Graphic was the camera of choice for White House photographers. Actually,

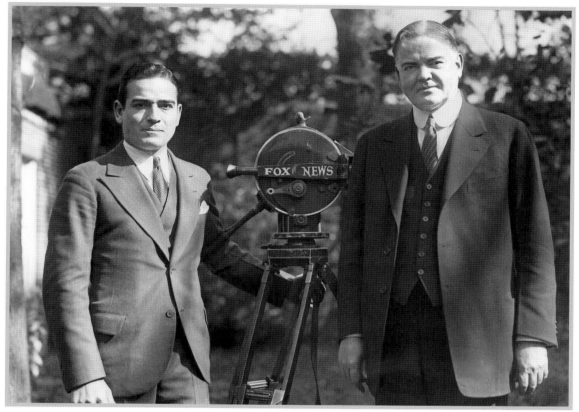

President Herbert Hoover with a Fox News cameraman.

before President Roosevelt got to the White House, the rules for photographers were already very clear: no pictures of the president on crutches or of him struggling into or out of a vehicle. Steve Early reiterated to the photographers that if they followed these rules, they'd get their pictures. By and large the photographers did follow the rules, but many times they didn't get their pictures. Roosevelt often left the photographers sitting at the White House during his secret trips. They knew he was not there, but they waited anyway.[1]

The Roosevelt White House years were hardly an era of candid photojournalism. Flash bulbs, then an innovation, bothered the president's eyes, so Steve Early issued orders that pictures would be made only when he said "shoot."[2] But old newsletters in the files of the White House News Photographers Association prove that the photographers liked President Roosevelt, in spite of the strict rules and his leaving them behind. According to one account:

Johnny Thompson's famous shot of President Franklin D. Roosevelt signing the declaration of war against Japan, December 8, 1941, at his desk in the Oval Office.

President Harry S. Truman, escorted by his press secretary, Eben Ayers, walks across Pennsylvania Avenue to the Old Executive Office Building on August 25, 1950, for his regular Wednesday press conference. He was living at that time in Blair House while his renovations of the White House were under way.

It was seldom that they entered his office that they were not greeted by a cheerful President Roosevelt. The president knew only a few photographers by name. One of his favorites was Johnny Thompson of Acme. Johnny was a tricky fellow. He would wait until all the other photographers had made their picture and, while they were busy changing film holders, quickly ask the president to do something that would make a much better picture. When Roosevelt signed the declaration of war with

BETTMANN/CORBIS, COURTESY OF THE HARRY S. TRUMAN LIBRARY

After being presented with a still camera by the White House News Photographers Association, President Harry Truman made them pose for a group portrait. Here Truman is seen taking the picture.

Japan, the photographers swarmed into the office to photograph the signing. Sure enough, they got their first shot picture and were changing holders on the Graphics. Johnny, who didn't shoot that first holder, asked Secretary Stimson, who was holding his pocket watch to get the exact time, to lean in closer to the president during the signing. Johnny's picture was the one that made the papers the next morning.[3]

The leisurely schedule of White House photographers covering the last of the Roosevelt years changed abruptly in the spring of 1945 to brisk early morning walks. President Harry S. Truman made a rule that any photographer who covered his constitutional also had to walk the entire way. The Truman White House was paradise for photographers. President Truman had been a friend of the photographers since he was a U.S. senator and vice president, and, as I gather, the photogra-

The picture President Truman took.

phers were his type of fellows. For Truman there were no structured photo-ops as we know them. The photographers would go into the Oval Office, perhaps move the subjects around to make the picture, and they would determine when they had enough. The senior photographer would end the session by saying, "Thank you Mr. President." President Truman would reply, "Are you sure?" And someone would say, "Well, maybe one more?" The "Just One More Club" was born.[4] President Truman loved his club, and when he was on trips often he would point to the photographers and tell people, "I have a club over at the White House known as the One More Club. I am the president of the club and these fellows all belong to it." One Sunday morning President Truman called all of the photographers together on the South Lawn, and he actually took our picture!

On November 1, 1950, when assassins attempted to enter Blair House, where President Harry Truman and his family were living, bullets rained for a moment, taking the life of one of the White House police. This image captures the moments that followed the gunfire.

About lunchtime on November 1, 1950, five photographers were getting into a car to cover the president at a ribbon-cutting ceremony at Arlington Cemetery. Truman was living in Blair House. All of a sudden there were gunshots. The five ran to Blair House and saw a Secret Serviceman—a friend—fatally wounded, lying on the sidewalk. The photographers made one holder; then, when they looked up, they saw President Truman looking down from the second-story window. By the time they got the holders flipped, the Secret Service had jerked the president inside to safety. Nobody recorded that memorable instant.

When Dwight David Eisenhower moved in to the White House, Washington photographers had a new tool, the Rolleiflex—a great camera but slow to work, so the photographers simplified the process by adding a control knob that set the

BETTMANN/CORBIS

President Dwight D. Eisenhower often practiced his golf swing on the South Lawn. Here he is seen on February 19, 1953, with his caddy, John Moaney.

camera at six feet, ten feet, and twenty feet without need to look through the lens to focus. Ike had a new camera, too—a Stereo Realist. For the photographers, these were not the great times of the Truman years, but they weren't bad. Ike knew that posing for photographs was part of the job, and he complied. But photographers were once again shooting pictures through the iron rods of the White House fence—this time to catch the president practicing his golf.

Recently I talked with Arnie Sacks, one of our members who covered the Eisenhower years, and he said that Ike would pretend he didn't know you when he really did. Arnie says the good times photographers had with Eisenhower were due to the skills of his press secretary Jim Hagerty, an advance man before there were advance men. One time Ike went hunting with a congressman in Alabama, and

President John F. Kennedy in his office in the heat of the Cuban crisis, facing another kind of heat.

they shot a lot of "chuckers"—little birds, probably doves. Hagerty told the photographers to make sure to be at the White House at one o'clock on a certain Thursday. Everyone showed up, and they were invited up to the State Dining Room for a lunch of the chuckers—cooked by the White House staff.

Again technology and the times were changing the makeup of the organizations covering the White House. For thirty years Harris & Ewing had a man at the White House, but this firm could no long compete with the wires. There was one less photographer among the regulars, but not for long. *Life* magazine had often sent photographers to cover the White House but had never assigned one full time. This being the era of the cold war, a contingency plan was formed for the evacuation of the president to a Maryland mountain bomb shelter in the event of a nuclear attack. It was made known that a small pool from the press corps would go along. *Life,* of course, wanted to be in that pool, so the magazine started sending a photographer to cover the White House every day. Hagerty finally deemed *Life* a "regular," and the magazine's photographer came into the pool.

The 35-mm camera shop and President John F. Kennedy dramatically changed the way photographers covered the White House. President Kennedy would permit a photographer to remain close to him and shoot available-light photographs as he went about his day. We called it being "in the closet" because you would sit in Evelyn Lincoln's closetlike office adjacent to the Oval Office and quietly venture from there into the Oval Office, make a few pictures, then go back to the closet and wait. We all know that one photographer didn't sit quietly during his closet days. The affable George Tames of the *New York Times Magazine* would swap gossip, tell jokes, and then every once in a while make a great picture. Nobody knew his craft better than George Tames. The years at the Kennedy White House were quite short. I think of them as having closed with the famous *Life* cover photograph by Fred Ward.

One thing that makes behind-the-scenes coverage possible is the depth of understanding that Washington photographers have of their subjects. Washington photographers report with their pictures, not with words. Very often a reporter will ask, "What did they say in there, what went on?" and the photographer will just answer, "Didn't hear a thing. I was too busy taking pictures."

Lyndon Johnson dealt with everyone personally, even the photographers. Charlie Gory will never forget his conversation with Johnson the day after he made his famous picture of LBJ pulling on his dogs' ears. Johnson reasoned with Charlie. "Charlie, why'd you take a picture like that? Don't you ever take a picture

The Rose Garden wedding of Tricia Nixon, daughter of President and Mrs. Richard M. Nixon, and Edward Cox, June 12, 1971.

like that again." Although he wasn't a member of the White House News Photographers Association during the LBJ years, I have to mention Yoichi Okamoto. He was the first official White House photographer and was by far the greatest of all the official White House photographers. He was a very strong man and one of the few people who stood up to President Johnson. He would do the job only if he was given complete access to the president. He used his privilege wisely and created a brilliant visual library of the Johnson years.

A major event at the White House during these years was the daughter Lynda Bird's wedding. Both the wedding and reception took place inside the White House and were highly lit for television and still-photo coverage. Actually, it took

President Lyndon B. Johnson's beagles, Him and Her, gave him great pleasure and a lot of news coverage, some of it unwanted.

President Jimmy Carter favored a populist image and carried his own briefcase. He is seen here between the helicopter and the White House, sprinting over the South Lawn.

COURTESY OF THE JIMMY CARTER LIBRARY

all the lights the equipment rental companies in Washington could provide, and they had to be painted white to match the decor. To this day, when you rent lighting, as the networks do, you encounter some of those same spots and queens with traces of white paint.

The Nixon administration gets the dubious credit for the first photo-op, and a great deal of our coverage of that administration was by controlled picture events. It was our challenge to get from what we saw some feel of what was really happening during these photo-ops. Again we were shooting pictures with long lenses from the wrong side of the White House fence. The final day of the Nixon administration produced the most memorable pictures. Every photographer on the South Lawn that August day remembers just how many frames he or she had left when Richard M. Nixon left the White House.

In spite of all the photographs catching him off balance, President Ford had a very warm relationship with the photographers. There is no doubt that these photographs hurt his chances for reelection, but President Ford went out of his way to help us. He was too big a man to hold a grudge. Very soon after President Ford moved into the White House he made David Kennerly of *Time* the White House photographer, and Kennerly readily helped any photographer who had a good idea for a picture. Dick Swanson of *People* wanted to take a picture from the bottom of the White House swimming pool of President Ford doing his daily exercises, and he did.

PLATE 20

Things were a little different for our members during the Carter years. The honeymoon period lasted until about two o'clock on the president's first day in the Oval Office. President Jimmy Carter was to make his first outing. The pool was prepositioned to make the photograph of President Carter confidently striding down the walk with the Oval Office in the background. But a tiny piece of ice changed all of this. President Carter didn't fall to the ground, but the photograph of him slipping was on the front pages of just about every newspaper the next day.

The Carter people never understood photographers and the value of having the cooperation of photographers. Very few pictures were ever taken above the state floor of the White House. As it was, the best photograph was taken from the ground anyway. The White House News Photographers are friends and work together, but they are competitors. One day two wire service photographers were walking back to the press room after lunch, and one spotted Amy Carter reading a book, but he just kept walking. He didn't say a thing. The two went into the press room, and the other photographer went to call his desk. The first photographer eased back outside and made the picture.

PLATE 21

Ronald Reagan was the photographer's dream president. He was a great subject, and editors knew that their readers wanted to see pictures of this president. The people in the Reagan administration were interested in producing good photographs to get their message across. They knew the best way to get a great picture was to ask the photographers just where a great picture was likely to happen and then get them in position to take that picture. The photographers were in love

PLATE 22

with Nancy Reagan. Many of the photographers traveled with the Reagans for two campaigns, so they were good friends. I will never forget one evening at a White House event. Mrs. Reagan looked just stunning, and the pool must have shown approval through a blitz of strobes, because Mrs. Reagan turned and in a very soft voice said, "Come on boys, it's only me."

President George Bush called the photographers the "photo dogs," and almost every morning on his way to the Oval Office he would walk down the colonnade and up the ramp into the press office, and stick his head in the press briefing room and ask the wire service photographers (the only ones there at that early hour), "How are you photo dogs doing today?" Every summer he would have a picnic on the South Lawn for about thirty still photographers and their wives or dates— good times for the photo dogs.

The Clinton years are a good place to end up because they have many of the elements of the previous administrations. Bill Clinton was an excellent subject, a showman with a smart staff who knew how to work with photographers. Behind-the-scenes access was granted at times. At other times there was the challenge of an embattled White House, when you'd have to tell the story with only limited glimpses of the president.

PLATE 23

Finally, technology advanced once again. Cameras using glass plates the size of 5- by 7-inch windowpanes evolved to film the size of postage stamps, and now most of the photographers covering the White House are using cameras that use no film at all. Today a photographer will photograph the president walking from the Oval Office to the press room and on a laptop computer select an image and send it instantly. Surely future members of the White House News Photographers will smile at this ancient technology; nevertheless, the speed and format of the images are not what is important. We will still be telling stories with our pictures.

Membership in the White House News Photographers Association has grown over the years. The open press coverage by numbers of photographers on major events has been accommodated by imaginative advance offices. Today every Oval Office event is a pool situation. A great deal of effort is spent on just who will be in this pool and in what order they will enter the Oval Office. This is a far cry from the fellows who wandered into the Oval Office during the Truman years. But it is better than being on the curb of West Executive Avenue.

NOTES

1. George Tames, *Eye on Washington* (New York: Harper Collins, 1990), 20.

2. Howard L. Kany and William C. Bourne, *Dateline: Washington* (Garden City, N.Y.: Doubleday, 1949), 150–51.

3. A. L. Scott, "Twenty-Five Years of Growing Pains," *White House News Photographers Association Annual* (Washington, D.C.: WHNPA, 1956), 9.

4. Tom O'Halloran, Harris & Ewing, interview with author, 1960s.

Pebble Beach, the White House roost of TV news reporters.

Presidential Reality
"If It Hasn't Happened on Television, It Hasn't Happened"

MARTHA JOYNT KUMAR

TELEVISION is a presence presidents fear and favor. Whether they are on the campaign trail or governing, chief executives and those who work for them view television as both an opportunity and a hazard. They welcome television to the White House as a resource, but, at the same time, they are wary of the medium, knowing it can serve as an effective weapon in the hands of a president's opponents. Making the most of television is difficult for a president because the organizations that constitute the medium define for themselves their criteria of what constitutes a story and what issues, actions, and people should be covered by their reporters.

News slips out of the White House at what seems like lightning speed. In July 1996, on the morning following the crash of TWA Flight 800 in Long Island Sound, Press Secretary Mike McCurry held his morning meeting with reporters and provided them with President Bill Clinton's response to the plane crash. The meeting lasted its normal fifteen minutes or so. As reporters walked from the press secretary's office following the session, they passed through the lower press office, where on the television set they could see CNN's senior White House correspondent, Wolf Blitzer, wrapping up his report. McCurry gave the presidential response at the top of the session, and then Blitzer went out on the North Lawn, to "pebble beach," where the TV cameras are set up, and gave his report. It took less than five minutes.

When White House personnel want to get a story about the president and his policies into the news bloodstream, television has the capacity to spread their information rapidly. At the same time, presidents and those who work for them have found that bad news travels just as quickly as good news. To make the most effec-

DENNIS BRACK

President Bill Clinton's press secretary, Mike McCurry, at a press briefing in the White House Press Room, West Wing.

tive use of television at the White House, most recent presidents have created a communications operation that takes advantage of the opportunities while also providing rapid response to unfavorable news stories.

Television as a presence chief executives have to deal with dates back to the Truman administration, but only recently have news organizations had the capacity to go live throughout the day. Nearly forty years ago, President Lyndon Johnson was interested in having a regular White House presence for the camera, but at that time the networks claimed it took them six hours to arrange a broadcast from the White House.[1] The long lead time did not dissuade the president. "Once Johnson went on the air so fast," an NBC executive recalled, "that we couldn't put up the presidential seal. When a network technician said we need a second to put up the presidential seal, Johnson said: 'Son, I'm the leader of the free world, and I'll go on the air when I want to.'"[2] For presidents, television is not only a vehicle and a presence; it has become its own reality. Speaking from the White House point of view, Ron Nessen, Gerald Ford's press secretary, once said, "If it hasn't happened on television, it hasn't happened."[3] Another official of the Ford White House explained, "You pitch everything you have at television."[4] Democrats and Republicans alike have followed the dictum.

In the latter half of the twentieth century, television grew from a rarity to a regular presence in almost every household in the country. While in the middle of the Truman administration only 9 percent of U.S. households had a television set, 87 percent had TVs by the end of the Eisenhower administration and 95 percent early in the Nixon administration.[5] In the course of those five decades, presidents and their staffs have learned to use the medium to achieve their personal and policy ends. At the same time, chief executives have found that, just as often, television has an impact on them. This essay focuses primarily on the manner in which presidents use television to govern and the way in which chief executives are shaped by it.

Historically, presidents have used the latest technology to reach the public, whose support and trust they need. Presidential use of television fits into a well-established pattern. Even in the earliest days, presidents were interested in communicating with citizens through whatever means were available.

In the eighteenth and nineteenth centuries, presidents took circuit visits around the country, called "swings-around-the-circle," to promote their policies and programs. They and those who worked for them always made certain to use the latest technology to get the president where he was going and to broadcast desirable information in as wide a circle as possible. When President Grover Cleveland took a three-week trip to the Midwest and South, including stops in Indi-anapolis, St. Louis, Minneapolis, Sioux City, Nashville, Atlanta, and Montgomery, reporters were with him on the train. In his account of the 1887 trip, the president's private secretary, Colonel Daniel S. Lamont, noted there were ten people in their party, including the president and Mrs. Cleveland as well as representatives of two press associations and an artist.[6] All three were important for publicity purposes. The United Press and Associated Press representatives could describe the trip to those who would miss its passage through their towns, and the artist's sketches, made aboard the train, were widely reprinted. In his summary Lamont jotted in his trip notes: "During the three weeks of his journey they traveled 4500 miles, passed through 17 states, crossing three of them twice, and the President has been seen by (variously estimated by different members of the party at from one to five million) of American citizens."[7] In a United States of between 50 and 60 million people, that is a large percentage.[8] Lamont then added comically: "On leaving Memphis the train went several miles before it was discovered that the President and Mrs. Cleveland were not aboard." So the train was, necessarily, "backed up to the sta-tion."[9]

When one considers the local exposure generated by the president's visit, the publicity value of such trips was substantial. Artist's sketches were replaced by pho-tographs when photography became a feature of newspapers, and the president's staff members eagerly incorporated it into their plans. In his papers in the Library of Congress, George Cortelyou, a presidential assistant who served as secretary to Presidents William McKinley and Theodore Roosevelt, listed press representatives for the April 29–June 15, 1901, trip President McKinley took to the West Coast.[10] Among the many press people on the trip—ten of the forty-four people in the presidential party—was a photographer.[11] A patron of the gifted photographer Frances Benjamin Johnston, Cortelyou worked hard to convince President and Mrs. McKinley to sit for their portraits, which were widely published.[12] Be it by artist or photographer, the president's staff was anxious to make use of the latest technology to get the chief executive's image to the public.

Radio came to be a part of the presidency in much the same way as photog-raphy. In 1924 the party conventions were reported on radio. Shortly before the election, President Calvin Coolidge used radio to deliver a speech from the White House. It was broadcast nationwide on twenty-seven stations.[13] The following year Coolidge's inaugural address was also broadcast. Radio became a distinctive feature of the presidency with President Franklin D. Roosevelt and was welcomed by his

A White House press conference, with familiar faces in the crowd: Sam Donaldson, ABC; Helen Thomas, UPI; Scott Pelley, CBS; Wolf Blitzer, CNN.

successors. The move from radio to television was equally swift, although the impact of television was stronger.

Television was first used at the White House—foreshadowing how the medium is used today—as an instrument to further a policy as well as to showcase the president advocating it. The first broadcast using the cathode ray took place on October 5, 1947, and launched a food-saving campaign for relief abroad. It featured comments by the head of the relief effort, corporate executive Charles Luckman, and by Secretary of State George C. Marshall, Secretary of Agriculture Clinton Anderson, Averell Harriman, and President Harry S. Truman.[14] In 1949, Truman's inaugural address was televised.

The first really important use of television as a leadership tool was on July 20, 1950, when President Truman went to the public at the beginning of the Korean War. Jack Gould, a radio and television critic at the *New York Times,* made the following observation in his column: "President Truman's appearance on television last night will be remembered. For the first time in a period of national emergency, the person at home not only heard the fateful call for sacrifices to preserve his freedom, but also saw the grave expressions of the President as he explained to the country what it would mean. In millions of living rooms . . . history was personalized last night."[15]

Even before it moved into the White House on a permanent basis, television had an impact on presidential elections. It was used, first, to broadcast presidential nominating conventions. Then it was used for campaign advertisements, for speeches, and finally for presidential debates. The 1948 conventions were televised, not nationally but on the East Coast, where television stations were based. In 1952 Dwight Eisenhower used television ads for his campaign, and the Republican vice presidential candidate, Richard Nixon, televised his "Checkers" speech, reaching out to the public to save his political career and retain his place on the ticket. In 1956, through the Republican National Committee, President Eisenhower brought in the public relations firm of Batten, Barton, Durstine & Osborn (BBDO) to help in the reelection effort. Targeting women, the firm televised coffees with Eisenhower supporters to win the female vote. The 1960 presidential campaign added televised debates to the electoral mix, though they did not become a permanent feature until 1976.

Since 1952, television has proved central to all presidential campaigns. When Ronald Reagan ran in 1980, his political team made certain his staff understood the importance of television to their goal of presenting their candidate to the voting public. Television was central to everything they did. The advance book distributed to key campaign officials described the role of television this way: "Your ability to obtain a prime spot for TV and press photographers will make the difference between mediocre TV and news photo coverage and first-rate coverage. Remember: *The coverage opportunity is why the candidate is there in the first place.*"[16]

As presidents have campaigned, so have they governed. The presidents who used television to get elected also used it to communicate their presidencies. Lessons learned on the campaign trail are incorporated by the president and his staff into their governing style. In a system that Richard Neustadt refers to as "separated institutions sharing power,"[17] presidents have used their relations with the public to solidify their leadership—personal, electoral, and institutional. Presidents and their staffs seek throughout each term of office to strengthen the chief executive's relationship with the public, and television is particularly well adapted to their needs. In a mere half-century, from its beginning in the Truman administration when it was a vehicle for occasionally going to the public, to our time when it is deeply woven into the fabric of the contemporary presidency, television has become a tradition.

Television was seen from the start as an effective tool for a president to use in marking his brand of leadership. The State of the Union Address took on added significance once television carried it. Presidents have come to count on this speech as the most important one they deliver all year. Because people do watch it and listen to what the president has to offer, the speech has become the policy focal point for the president, his cabinet officers, and his advisers. Ann Lewis, communications director for President Bill Clinton, described how the president's 1997 State of the Union address drove his agenda for the coming year:

> You will have a State of the Union Address which will include much of our agenda for the year, and a lot of what we do during the year is then live up to, carry out, implement, follow through on that State of the Union. . . . I'm not saying we succeeded in them all [initiatives mentioned in the speech], but we had follow-through on most of them and succeeded on a great many. We have succeeded on a great many and we followed up on all of them, made some effort. So that, in a way, the State of the Union provides your agenda, a big piece of it. The address itself and many of the ceremonies involving initiatives mentioned in it are carried by television throughout the year.[18]

In our time presidents regularly use television to present their case to the public. President Clinton's address in the East Room on October 1, 1997, is an example. The issue was global warming, and the event was a speech to television weather forecasters who were invited to the White House for a day of briefings. At the end of the day there were speeches by the president and vice president. President Clinton discussed the difficulty of getting our society to respond to issues and how important it was for the president to create public awareness of them and, by implication, the important role of television in getting him—and the weather forecasters—into the citizens' living rooms with discussions of the issues. The following is a direct quotation:

> What I want to do is deal with the central political problem here—and I don't mean political in terms of party politics; I mean political in terms of how the body politic, how our society, responds to this—if we have a problem that is a clear and present danger that we can see and feel, we can get right on it. How did we get to the moon? Because the Russians beat us into space, so we knew how to keep score, we would beat them to the moon. . . . Now, it is much harder when you have no manifestation of this problem unless you happen to live in a place which has experienced an unusual number of or intensity of aberrations. . . . This is a case where people need the facts and the context, where if all you do is just try to get people to start thinking about this. . . . We always get it right once we focus on it. But right now, while the scientists see the train coming through the tunnel, most Americans haven't heard the whistle blowing. They don't sense that it's out there as a big issue. And I really believe, as president, one of my most important jobs is to tell the American people what the big issues are that we have to deal with. If we understand what the issues are, if we start with a certain set of principles, we nearly always come to the right place. . . . But we can't do it until we build the awareness of the American people.[19]

Building awareness is what television can do for presidents, and contemporary chief executives have communications operations organized to contrive opportunities and stage events specifically for television. Once presidents learned to employ television to win the presidency, they became increasingly comfortable using it to govern.

To effectively use television to serve their policy, electoral, and personal goals, presidents and their staffs have created organizations to handle their relations to it. These organizations establish rules that govern the presence of cameras in the White House, and once favorable rules are established, the president and his staff make every effort to maintain their advantage.

The Eisenhower White House was the first to weave television into its presidential politics and to create an organization to advise on communications matters. Eisenhower's press secretary, James Hagerty, saw television as a way of getting the president to the public without the filter of print and magazine reporters. In his

President Bill Clinton meeting with journalists in the Roosevelt Room before his trip to Japan and Korea, July 1993.

diary entry of March 4, 1954, he wrote, "To hell with slanted reporters, we'll go directly to the people who can hear exactly what Pres [Eisenhower] said without reading warped and slanted stories."[20] In addition to Hagerty, President Eisenhower brought in experts to advise on how to deal with the new medium. Robert Montgomery, an actor and active Eisenhower supporter during the 1952 campaign, came to the White House in December 1953 to discuss technical issues as well as the character of the appearances the president should establish.[21] He advised the president and his staff to arrange "fireside chats" in the manner of FDR's radio addresses, using television instead of radio. Eisenhower delivered the first chat later that month, at Christmas, making use of the South Lawn of the White House instead of a fireplace. In this chat, the president combined a special occasion with family and presidential politics. He reviewed the blessings of the nation at this time when troops were returning from Korea, inflation was down, and economic stability was responsible for an increased number of jobs.

Presidents Nixon and Reagan further developed the White House communications apparatus. The Office of Communications was established by President Nixon to reach news organizations outside of the Washington community, including television in regional and local areas. President Reagan enhanced this office by organizing the booking of guests on Sunday talk programs as well as preparing talking points for those appearing. The Public Affairs Office spelled out recent administration successes for the surrogates to use.

In addition, the Reagan White House set up a television studio in the Old Executive Office Building for use by the president and staff. An example of its value came when top White House staff used it to advance the Supreme Court nomination of Robert Bork. Chief of Staff Howard Baker appeared on local television programs, via the studio, to answer questions about the nomination. He did the presentations seriatim, moving from one television program to another as a White House staff member held up a sign indicating the names of the anchors and the location of the program.[22]

While not all presidents have created a well-oiled communications apparatus, and Presidents Jimmy Carter and George Bush chose not to do so, the Clinton administration built a masterpiece indeed. The Clinton staff found such an organization a necessity because of the difficulty in getting today's public to focus on national politics. Ann Lewis described how the staff encouraged television coverage by tailoring events to meet the interests, needs, and timing of news organizations. The public wants to "know what you're doing and check in from time to time," she said, but to claim the attention of the public requires the cooperation of the president, television, and an organized White House staff. Lewis observed that the most effective way to reach people

> has clearly been to see and hear the president of the United States talking about issues they care about, that resonate with their lives. So our job is to make that happen as often as we can. What you have to do is talk to people directly, but remember the number of people who are going to read the *New York Times* is a lot smaller than the number of people who see television. So you spend a lot of time figuring out how you can get into the news, on television. Direct communication is going to be stronger, closer to what you have in mind, and certainly resonates a lot more with the public. Our goal would be to look for a message, then, that will break through [and] be reported a couple times a week. You do that, that would be success.[23]

Thomas Griscom, communications director in the White House during Ronald Reagan's second term and a former press secretary to Senate Majority Leader Howard Baker, captures the modern White House communications operation in the following description. What the White House did, even before the Reagan administration, was

> set up a PR industry inside the White House . . . that is like having a full service public affairs department. That's really what you have got. Think about what has been brought in. Extensive polling, to help you set message points, audiences to reach, what the potential negative or downside is of an issue, then all the vehicles that you want to have established to help you get that message out—politically, interest group wise, public media, whatever. It really becomes like a public relations firm. . . . You got an inside studio where you could go in and weed out your news clips and all these kind of things, like a full-fledged operation.[24]

Defining the message and identifying the people giving it are central to the communications strategies of the White House. In staging an event, White House communicators identify five items: what the President says, where and how he says it, who the audience is, what the picture is, and what the headline is. For events such as the speech to TV weather forecasters that addressed the global warming issue, White House staff try to provide reporters with words and pictures for television as well as their "lede." Ann Lewis, who as a White House aide set up these events, laid out the ingredients by saying, "Whenever we can, when you see the president at an event, there will be a graphic nearby that states the case in six words or eight words or less. So in a sense his speech is the text of a story. We've got the text, we've got the headline, we've got the lead, and if we can, we've provided the picture." Central to the mix is the policy itself. "They're only going to make it, though, with a strong policy component," she said, "a strong policy component and a sense of what policy it is [is what] the networks are interested in at that time."[25] Another aide explained that getting on television is linked to an ability to divine what the networks are interested in at any given moment. "Something has to be clued in to something that they're interested in at the moment—child care, families, kids, something they're interested in right now. Education. For a while there the environment was huge . . . during the campaign, ABC was huge on the environment."[26]

Such efforts within the White House rely upon outside as well as inside re-

sources. In addition to the Office of Communications, the Press Office, the domestic, economic, and national security shops are brought in to shape events, and
so are polling and political experts. While television itself represents a means
whereby the president can get help at little cost to his administration, the resources
a president has are surprisingly sparse. He is forced to forage for the resources of
others he might leverage to his benefit. This his communications staff helps him do
effectively. For President Clinton's global warming event, all the White House had
to provide were the risers for the cameramen to stand on. The cameras were provided by the networks, the lighting was maintained by the network assigned to that
role for that month, the White House Communications Agency ran the audio
lines, and the network technicians and cameramen laid the required cable.

The place of television events in the White House today is a result of innovations by President Clinton's predecessors who used television as a campaign and
governing tool and created an organization to develop events and opportunities
that could showcase the president and his administration. It is also the result of
pressure on the president and his staff from the use of television by others, including the many institutions, individuals, and governments using it to steer him and
his policies their way.

The president seeks to control when and under what circumstances television
cameras enter the White House and who makes use of the presidential image. This
is one of the controls Truman's and Eisenhower's successors have wished to extend.
When press conferences were informal events with reporters clustered around
Franklin D. Roosevelt's Oval Office desk, radio interviews twice a week worked
well. The president did not speak on the record, and there was no risk the public
would tire of him. Once television took over, press conferences became less frequent.
Increased public exposure of the president resulting from television coverage led to
new strategies to reduce the vulnerability brought on by the new medium. Press
conferences were once known as informal exchanges, but the coming of television
brought an organizational response from the White House staff that sought to control the presidential image.

Eisenhower's press secretary, James Hagerty, decided the time had come to put
press conferences on television, and he prepared the way by establishing new rules.
At the end of President Eisenhower's news conference on December 16, 1953,
Hagerty announced that the sessions would be no longer covered by a "no quotation" rule and that a tape recording would be released to the radio networks and
television. Reporters were allowed to quote from the transcripts as long as they
quoted from the transcripts Hagerty provided.[27] To open news conferences to tel-

evision, Hagerty worked with Kodak to develop lighting that would allow the president to be comfortable while he responded to questions. On January 19, 1955, Eisenhower's press conference was filmed for the first time for newsreels and for television. The rules stayed the same: Hagerty provided edited film to the networks.[28] The first live televised press conference came not from Kennedy, as people often think, but from Eisenhower, in San Francisco on August 22, 1956. Hagerty continued screening the sessions, but once Eisenhower became comfortable with them, the editing was omitted.[29] Now, before the president appears at a press conference, he receives a briefing book and then practices a run-through with staff.

While the chief executive and his staff most often think of television as a resource, TV has proven difficult for presidents and their staffs to control. The importance of television around the world and in the backyard of his opponents has left an imprint on the president as well. His electoral opponents, those in the Congress, and interest groups of every stripe have used television for their purposes. So have governments and others the world over seeking the support or enticing the involvement of the United States.

Television was instrumental in providing the citizenry with information on the Vietnam War and the Watergate episode, two events in our national life in which presidents did not want attention directed toward the White House. Presidents found that officials in other governmental institutions made use of television as did those working for political parties and interest groups. By the Nixon administration, television was a central component in the changed environment within which Washington politics took place.

In terms of policy, television has often proved to be a president's ally. Pictures of the use of violence by police against demonstrators in the civil rights struggle worked in favor of passage of major legislation. Television drove the issue. In 1957, when Arkansas Governor Orval Faubus refused to comply with an order of the Supreme Court to integrate Little Rock's Central High School, television made the incident a national drama. Television brought home to the American public an ever-more vivid portrait of what discrimination meant. Police violence in southern states broadcast across the nation produced growing support for stronger action by the federal government to bring about compliance with court orders. Montgomery, Selma, Birmingham—all created pictures that presidents responded to with action.

What was happening with television in other institutions was just as important for the presidency. The organized crime hearings chaired in Washington and New

York by Senator Estes Kefauver brought that medium to Congress. In 1954 the hearings on the army, chaired by Senator Joseph McCarthy, forced an important item onto the president's agenda. He was then forced to take action, something he did not want to do.

As television matured, the environment of Washington politics was gradually changing with the development of interest groups pressing for legislation in a variety of domestic social areas. Television became an integral part of the tactics these groups used to advance their cause. Demonstrations in Washington beginning with the civil rights March on Washington in 1963 and then later the marches against the Vietnam War were television events that got a great deal of attention.

During the Clinton years, interest groups actively used television advertising as a way of shaping public impressions of controversial issues, such as the president's health care proposal. At the end of Clinton's presidency, television ads sponsored by environmental, business, and legal groups were a common feature of programming in Washington. In 1995 President Clinton turned the tables on his opponents by using the television ad strategy himself as a way to give the impression that the Republicans in Congress were responsible for the shutdown of the government as they debated the budget with the president.

But just as television can enhance a president's power to promote his agenda, it can also increase his vulnerability. During the Monica Lewinsky scandal, President Clinton and his staff learned a lesson in how quickly and profoundly that same resource can send out the bad news, along with devastating pictures. Yet President Clinton survived the Lewinsky debacle in part through the communications operation that managed his presidential information. Every day Press Secretary Mike McCurry and those in the Clinton communications operation worked to provide an image of a president fully concentrating upon his job. The Office of Communications set up events each day highlighting a policy mentioned by him in the State of the Union Address and provided supporting players to lend authenticity to their claim. They tailored presidential information to conform to the news routines of television networks.

One area in which television has had a strong impact on the presidency relates to the increasing transparency of government. The impact of the medium on the presidency has enhanced this trend as the public has demanded to know about the processes of government and has depended upon television to bring them the information they seek. During World War II, reporters and officials gave the government the benefit of the doubt. Reporters were reluctant to say President Franklin Roosevelt might be lying. But in the U-2 spy plane incident during the Eisen-

DENNIS BRACK

President Bill Clinton speaks to the nation in the Rose Garden after the Senate declined to support the impeachment conviction handed down by the House of Representatives.

hower administration, after viewers were treated by the Soviets to pictures of U.S. pilot Francis Gary Powers even as the U.S. government was maintaining its initial story that the plane was a weather plane, not a surveillance plane, the public began to distrust the president and his version of events.

In 1964, when President Johnson said that we had no troops in the Dominican Republic, CBS News showed a correspondent in the Dominican Republic standing in front of U.S. troops. Such pictures had and continue to have a strong impact on the viewer.[30] The continuing TV coverage of the Vietnam War, in which indecision rather than victory was conveyed in the images, also had a major impact on the public view of the president and his ability to govern.

PLATE 18

People tend to believe what they see on television more than what they read in newspapers. Television carries the characteristic believability of film; an audience believes a movie, but will view a play as make-believe. In 1959 29 percent of the public found television the most believable of media, 32 percent found newspapers to be so, and 12 percent chose radio. In 1994 the relation between television and newspapers shifted, with 51 percent of those surveyed regarding television the most believable of media and 21 percent viewing newspapers as the more trustworthy.[31]

The ascendancy of television over newspapers in trustworthiness is reflected in the growing reliance of the public on television as the source of most news. In 1959 the public saw both television and newspapers as important sources of news, with 51 percent citing television and 57 percent mentioning newspapers. In 1994, 72 percent said television was the source of most of their news, while only 38 percent cited newspapers.[32] The people who in 1959 were viewing television and reading newspapers for their news fairly swiftly dropped newspapers for television. In 1967, 73 percent of adults in the United States read one newspaper each day, but by 1990 that number had fallen to 51 percent.[33] Most recently, since the Reagan administration, cable television has had an impact. In 1981, 25.2 percent of American households had cable television; in 1994 that number rose to 62.4 percent.[34] The interest of the White House in providing information to the new outlets is a direct reflection of their growing importance in the constellation of broadcast institutions.

The growing transparency of the presidency as well as of government itself has been intensified by television coverage of government institutions. The consequence is increased public interest in the president but, at the same time, a growing distrust of what the government says. In addition, special interest groups have developed their own strategies for using television. Institutional routines for handling television build upon precedents and continue to evolve. In the last half-century, the four presidents elected to a second term—of the ten who served during that time period—have been successful in their use of television. What those four presidents—Dwight Eisenhower, Richard Nixon, Ronald Reagan, and Bill Clinton—had in common were communications operations that recognized television as the chief resource used to define the president and his electoral and policy goals. These presidents had a staff of professionals who understood the rhythms and routines of news organizations and were able to create a regular series of events tied to policy nodes that focused on the president's policy issues and conformed to the needs of television. These presidents also employed people from inside and outside the government who understood public opinion, the media, and the strengths of the president.

While the president regards television as a resource, it is also a factor that shapes national and international politics. Two recent examples from our public life

DENNIS BRACK

An evening news reporter in front of the White House.

demonstrate the degree to which television has insinuated itself into our political fabric and shaped political outcomes the world over. In October 2000, in a popular uprising against a dictatorial government in the Ivory Coast, protesters stormed the television station in Abidjan and freed it in much the same way that, weeks before, a television station had been targeted in Belgrade, during the contested election there. A rebel in Abidjan told a *New York Times* reporter, "The mistake [General] Guei [Gay] made was to let us watch scenes from Belgrade."[35] Here in the United States, too, television has proved to be a crucial element in our recent—and continuing—election, though in a different way. Early in the morning after election day 2000, Vice President Al Gore called Texas Governor George W. Bush with a concession statement based not on vote totals but rather on television predictions of the election result. In these instances, we see how television is a critical element in our political life, including that of the president of the United States.

NOTES

1. David Wise, *The Politics of Lying: Government Deception, Secrecy, and Power* (New York: Vintage Books, 1973), 373–74.

2. Ibid.

3. Ron Nessen, quoted in Michael Baruch Grossman and Martha Joynt Kumar, *Portraying the President: The White House and the News Media* (Baltimore: Johns Hopkins University Press, 1981), 45.

4. Background interview, quoted ibid., 279.

5. Harold W. Stanley and Richard G. Niemi, *Vital Statistics on American Politics* (Washington, D.C.: Congressional Quarterly Press, 1995), 47.

6. Daniel S. Lamont, "Railroad Tour 1887," Daniel S. Lamont Papers, Manuscript Division, Library of Congress, Washington, D.C.

7. Daniel S. Lamont, "President Cleveland's Trip 1887," Lamont Papers.

8. "U.S. Population, 1790–1990," in Stanley and Niemi, *Vital Statistics on American Politics,* 348.

9. Lamont, "President Cleveland's Trip 1887," 5.

10. The trip did not go its full length as President McKinley's wife, who suffered from epileptic seizures, became ill, and the party returned early to Washington.

11. George B. Cortelyou, "President McKinley's 1901 Trip to the Pacific Coast," George B. Cortelyou Papers, Manuscript Division, Library of Congress.

12. See, for example, the exchange of correspondence between George Cortelyou and Frances Benjamin Johnston, including one letter from Johnston to Cortelyou on September 19, 1898, and his to her on June 26, 1900, and December 29, 1900, Cortelyou Papers and William McKinley Correspondence Files, Manuscript Division, Library of Congress.

13. F. W. Marbut, *News from the Capital: The Story of Washington Reporting* (Carbondale: Southern Illinois University Press, 1971), 210.

14. Elmer E. Cornwell Jr., *Presidential Leadership of Public Opinion* (Bloomington: Indiana University Press, 1965), 266.

15. Quoted ibid.

16. "Press Advance," chap. 18 of *Manual for Advance Representatives,* not paginated, author's documents collection. On its cover page is the following advice to advance representatives: "UNDER NO CIRCUMSTANCES SHOULD YOU EVER LET THIS MANUAL OUT OF YOUR SIGHT. Never give or even show a copy to the local committee or anyone else."

17. Richard E. Neustadt, *Presidential Power: The Politics of Leadership* (New York: John Wiley & Sons, 1960), 33–39.

18. Ann Lewis, interview with author, Washington, D.C., December 17, 1998.

19. President William J. Clinton, speech in the East Room of the White House, October 1, 1997.

20. James Hagerty, diary, March 4, 1954, James Hagerty Papers, Dwight D. Eisenhower Library, Abiline, Kansas.

21. Craig Allen, *Eisenhower and the Mass Media: Peace, Prosperity, and Prime-Time TV* (Chapel Hill: University of North Carolina Press, 1993), 26–27.

22. Elizabeth Board, interview with author, Washington, D.C., January 12, 1989.

23. Lewis interview.

24. Thomas Griscom, interview with author, Washington, D.C., October 2, 1995.

25. Lewis interview.

26. Barry Toiv, interview with author, Washington, D.C., March 27, 1998.

27. James E. Pollard, *The Presidents and the Press: Truman to Johnson* (Washington, D.C.: Public Affairs Press, 1964), 69.

28. Allen, *Eisenhower and the Mass Media,* 61–62.

29. James Deakin, *Straight Stuff: The Reporters, the White House, and the Truth* (New York: William Morrow, 1984), 65.

30. Jed Duvall, CBS correspondent, interview with author, Washington, D.C., October 6, 2000.

31. Stanley and Niemi, *Vital Statistics on American Politics,* 68.

32. Ibid. See also Stephen Ansolabehere, Roy Behr, and Shanto Iyengar, *The Media Game: American Politics in the Television Age* (New York: Macmillan, 1993), 42–47.

33. Ansolabehere, Behr, and Iyengar, *Media Game,* 43–44.

34. Stanley and Niemi, *Vital Statistics on American Politics,* 47.

35. "Popular Uprising Ends Rule of General in Ivory Coast," *New York Times,* October 26, 2000, A14.

Index

Page numbers given in *italics* indicate illustrations.
Numbers given in **bold** indicate color plates.